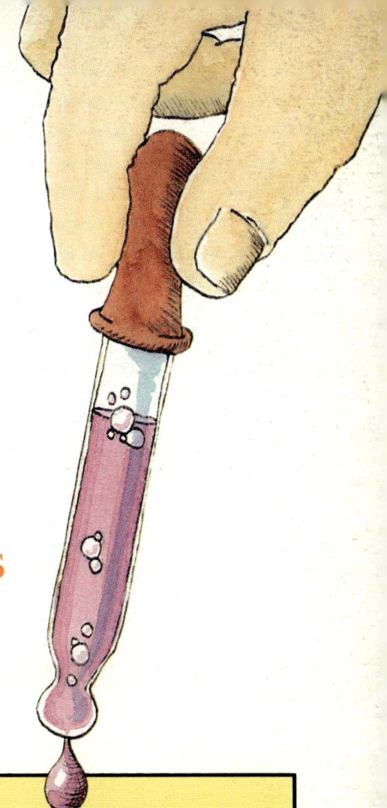

Larger than Life

Magnification from moulds to minibeasts

Beverley Birch

Contents

A window onto a miniature world 3

Making things larger than life 6

It's all in the lens 8

Planning and choosing 10

First steps forward 12

Using your microscope 14

A first look 16

Getting organized 18

Close to home 20

Better safe than sorry 22

Delving deeper 24

Experiments galore 30

The plant world 34

Into the outdoors 36

Further afield 40

All about lenses 42

Pushing back the frontiers of knowledge 44

Reference section 46

Index 48

Illustrated by Trevor Vincent

A & C Black · London

First published 1991
A & C Black (Publishers) Limited
35 Bedford Row, London WC1R 4JH

ISBN 0–7136–3469–3

A CIP catalogue record for this book is available from the British Library.

Acknowledgements
Photo credits:
pp 3, p 4 John Walsh Science Photo Library;
pp 8, 91 Microscopix;
p 9r Science Photo Library Dr T Brains & David Parker;
p 24–28 Nick Birch;
p 31 Microscopix;
p 32 Nick Birch;
p 33 Microscopix;
p 38 Robert Pickett;
p 44 Nick Birch;
p 45 Jenny Matthews.

Artwork by Trevor Vincent

Filmset by August Filmsetting, Haydock, St Helens
Printed and bound in Italy by Amadeus

A & C Black · London

FINDING OUT MORE

From time to time as you're reading **Larger than Life**, you'll see this symbol: ?? next to a list of subjects that you may want to find out more about. Underneath this list, you'll find the symbol →. It will be followed by suggestions for the headings to look out for in reference books and in your local library where you'll be able to find out more information about the ?? subjects.

A window onto a miniature world

There was once a man in Holland who made himself a magnifying glass and used it to peer at puddles in his yard. He didn't expect to see anything in particular – except, perhaps, to find out what rainwater looked like, close-up.

Imagine his amazement when, instead, he found himself gazing at millions of creatures darting through the water.

He took the lens away and looked with his naked eyes. Definitely nothing but water.

He peered through his lens again. Unmistakably, there were the creatures, wriggling and squirming and slithering, all endlessly busy.

Excited, he turned his lens on other things: fluid scraped from inside his mouth, his skin, tree-bark, leaves, the holes in rotten teeth. Everywhere he found these tiny energetic creatures – and they were always invisible until he revealed them with his lens!

He set about making other lenses, grinding and polishing each glass more carefully, making each lens more powerful – and he went on peering at anything within his reach.

There were no books to explain the creatures to him. No one else had ever seen them. But he wrote excited letters to other people, and they were caught by his enthusiasm and began their own explorations. And so the discoveries of one man in a quiet Dutch town about three hundred years ago launched the world on a scientific adventure that has still not ended.

This potato crisp has been magnified by a powerful piece of modern technology called an electron microscope. You can see the air-filled cavities which make it crunchy and the smoother, greasy surface.

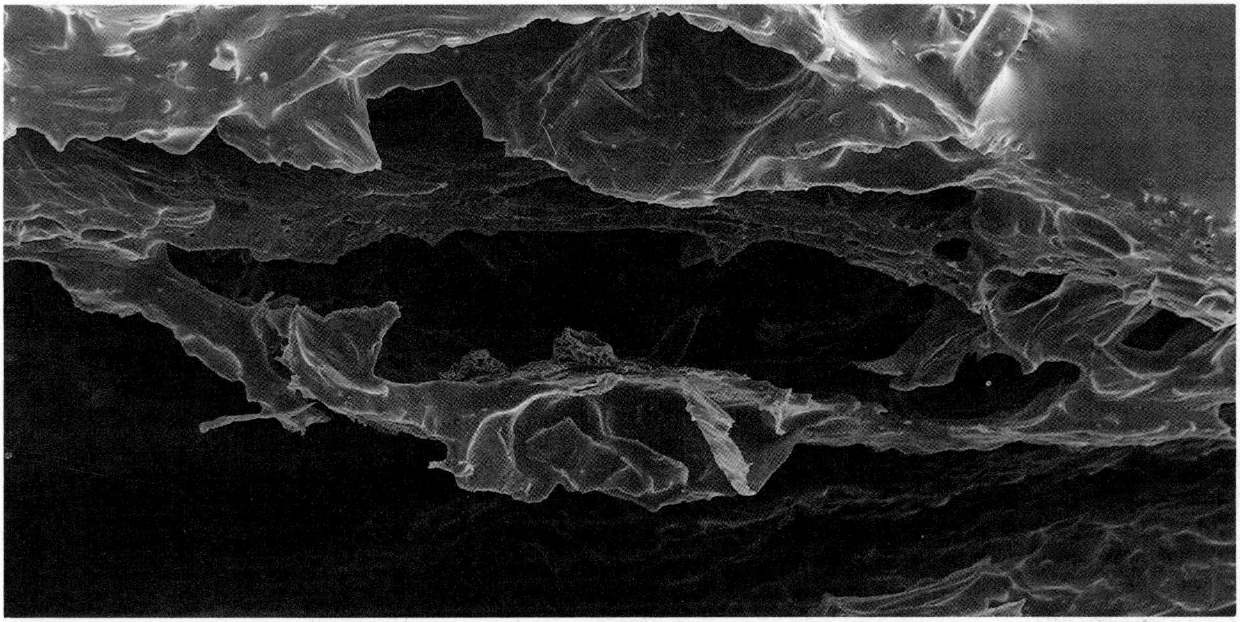

It is almost impossible to list all the benefits which flow from what we know about this tiny, hidden world. We first learned of it because one man simply wanted to know what things really looked like. His name was Antony van Leeuwenhoek; we remember him as one of the most important pioneers of the microscope.

Yet Leeuwenhoek was actually just like you might be, armed with your first lens, stepping outside to snoop under a leaf. He was just curious.

That is what this book is all about: curiosity. It is about you and your curiosity. This book will guide you, (armed with little more than an enquiring mind and a lens), towards your own explorations. Then you too can see into the vast, busy, useful – and sometimes dangerous – world usually hidden from you because you can see it only when you magnify it.

Weapons against disease

Over the last 300 years, lenses and microscopes have shown us much of what we now know about how things grow, decay and die. When Leeuwenhoek revealed the microscopic living world, people were at the daily mercy of scores of common, deadly diseases. Six thousand people might be carried off week after week, by diseases like the plague, cholera, typhoid, pneumonia and diphtheria.

No one understood why, and no one could prevent it.

But after Leeuwenhoek's microscope adventures, people had the key to change this. The lens showed them that Leeuwenhoek's tiny creatures were at the root of it all – of disease and decay and of many vital life processes on Earth. We could develop weapons against them and ways of using them to our benefit.

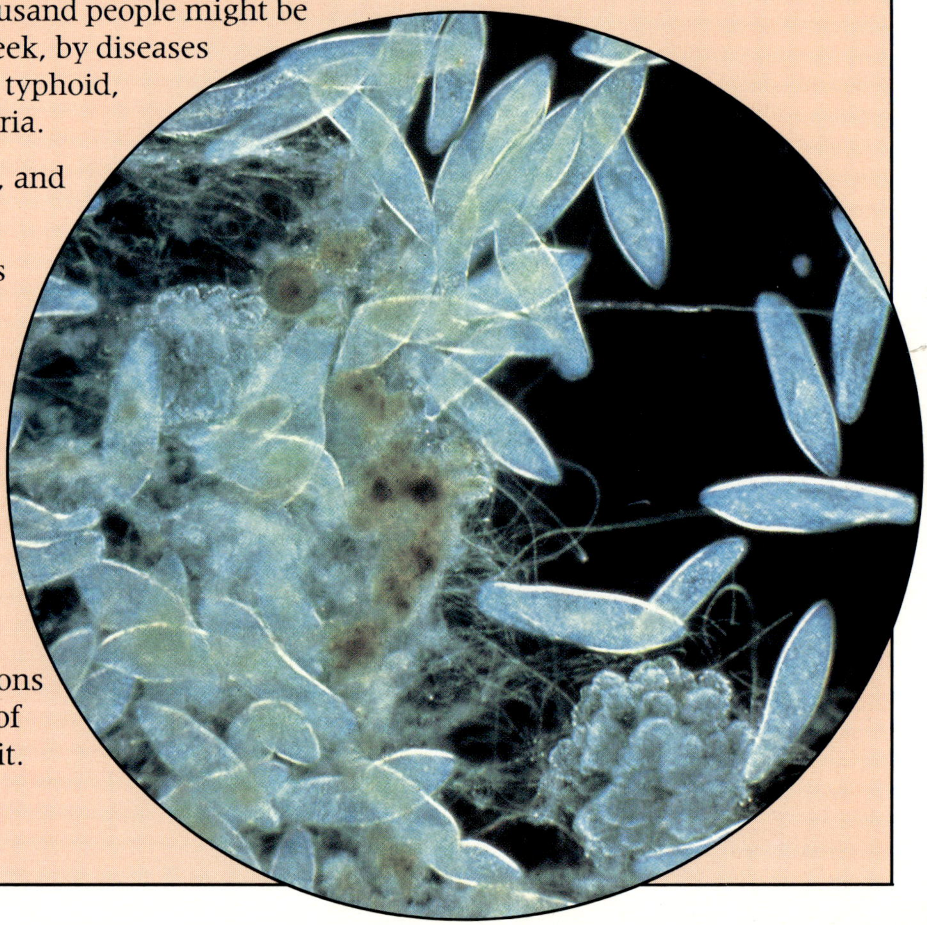

▼ *These are the kind of tiny living creatures that so excited Leeuwenhoek.*

Inner secrets

The microscope also gave us our first glimpse of the textures and structures of things. Here was the key to unlock age-old secrets about what makes up skin, blood and bone, plants and insects, rocks and soil.

Yet when you look back over the scientific advances of the past, you see that our enormous knowledge has come through many small, individual acts of curiosity and enquiry. People just like you became so absorbed by their explorations, that they followed their search for understanding to the end.

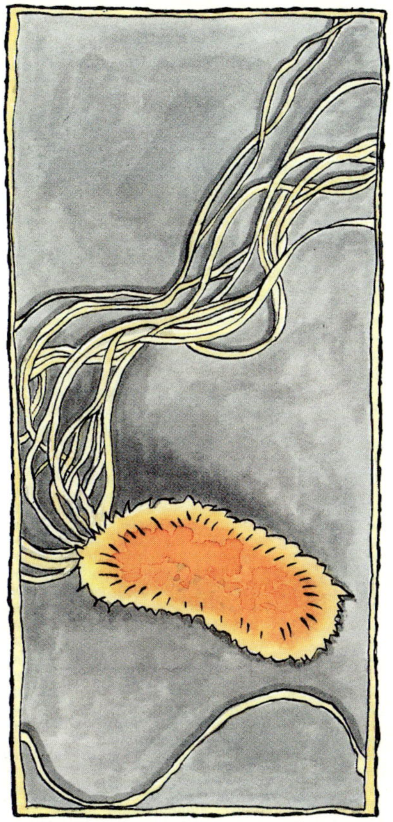

◀ *Microbes like this one live around your home in places where there is plenty of moisture such as damp sponges and dish cloths. The threads extending from the creature's body propel it along.*

Little by little each piece of information was added to every other, and so our wealth of scientific knowledge grew.

That is also what this book is about: how you can share the excitement of scientists throughout time. Pick up your lens and start to magnify the world around you: make it larger than life. And so begins your own scientific adventure.

▼ *Types of round, microscopic living creatures like these, called microbes, caused diseases like pneumonia and scarlet fever.*

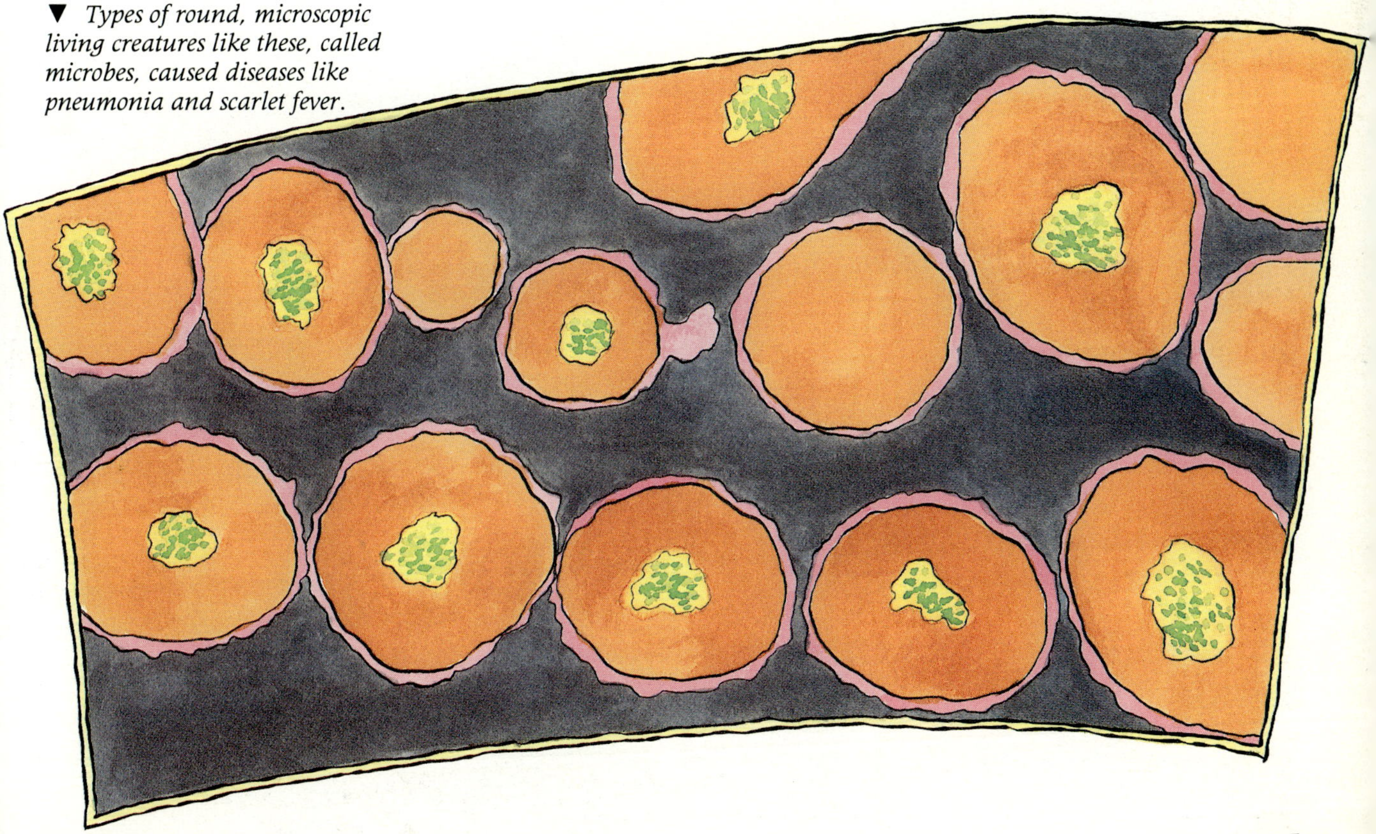

Making things larger than life

This book is about using magnifying lenses, from single hand-held lenses to the combination of lenses we call a microscope. On pages 42 and 43 you can find out how lenses work, but for now the important point is that magnifying lenses make things look larger.

This may help you to notice more detail on something you can already see, such as an insect or plant. You may be able to detect the fine details of its surface, how parts of it work, and the structure inside. The more powerful the lens, the more detail you will see. On the other hand you may use lenses to watch live insects and other tiny animals, or a seed pushing out shoots and a leafbud unfurling.

If you are able to magnify enough to see objects you would not see at all with your naked eye, you can also observe the minute life-forms called microbes. These are the tiny creatures that so excited Leeuwenhoek.

The lens that makes things look biggest isn't necessarily the best lens for a particular task. It all depends on what you want to see.

You may want to be a roamer, peering and poking (like Leeuwenhoek). Or you may want to be like the French scientist, Louis Pasteur. In Pasteur's hands the microscope was transformed. From a tool just for observing, it became one of the greatest weapons against disease. Pasteur had enormous imagination and energy. But he also had a determination to work steadily through any mystery, sorting and re-sorting the pieces of the puzzle until he had assembled every possible snippet of information.

Some of the lenses you can use:

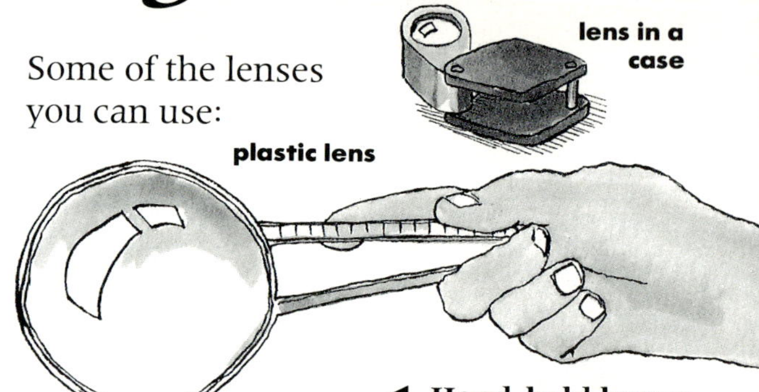

◄ **Hand-held lenses**
Hand lenses can make objects look three to ten times larger than their real size.

▼ **Magnifying boxes with lenses in the lids**
Some have a measuring grid so you can record the size of your object. They are useful for looking at small animals, insects, or liquid. The lenses have the same range of magnifying power as hand-held lenses. Stacking lids together can give extra magnification.

► **Magnifying glasses on stands**
Place the object underneath the stand. Look through the lens. Some have extra lenses for greater magnification.

◄ **Field microscopes**
These are light and portable inside cases, so you can carry them around easily without damaging the lenses.

Ordinary microscopes to use at home or school can magnify from 20 to 1200 times – but 2000 times is possible. A microscope can magnify more than a single glass because it combines two lenses. The first lens – the one closer to the object – is called the objective lens. It produces an enlarged image of the object, and this image is then magnified a second time by the upper lens – called the eye-piece. It is this second image which you see when you look through the microscope.

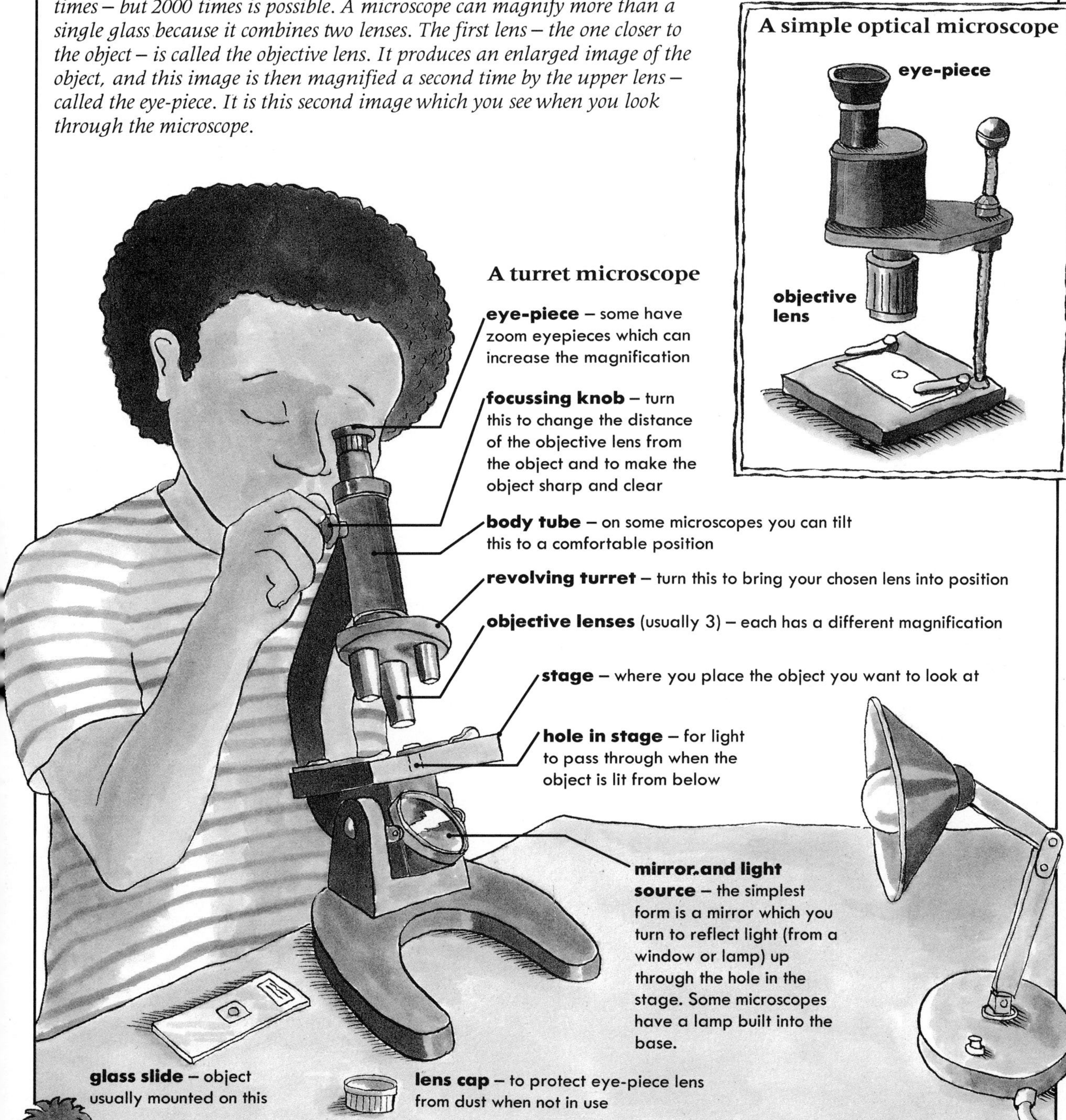

BEWARE KILLER SCIENTIST!

Never cause distress or harm to live creatures because of your investigations. For more about this see pages 10 and 11.

It's all in the lens

The smallest object your eye can see is about 0.1 millimetres long. Look at a ruler and work out how small this is. A fine pencil line is about 0.8 millimetres. So 0.1 millimetres is a barely visible dot.

It you magnify this to ten times its real size with a hand lens, you will get an image that you can see clearly – something about 1 millimetre in size.

If it is smaller than 0.1 millimetres, then you need to magnify it many more times to see anything. Anything this size is called microscopic – because it can be seen only with a microscope.

So, with a microscope you can see objects that are invisible to the naked eye. For example, you can see the basic units of living bodies, which we call cells. They are so tiny that there are about 50 billion in your body.

Yet with a microscope you can see the shape of a cell. With powerful lenses, you can see how the cell is made up of other, smaller parts. The wriggling creatures which Leeuwenhoek first saw are microscopic creatures of only one cell.

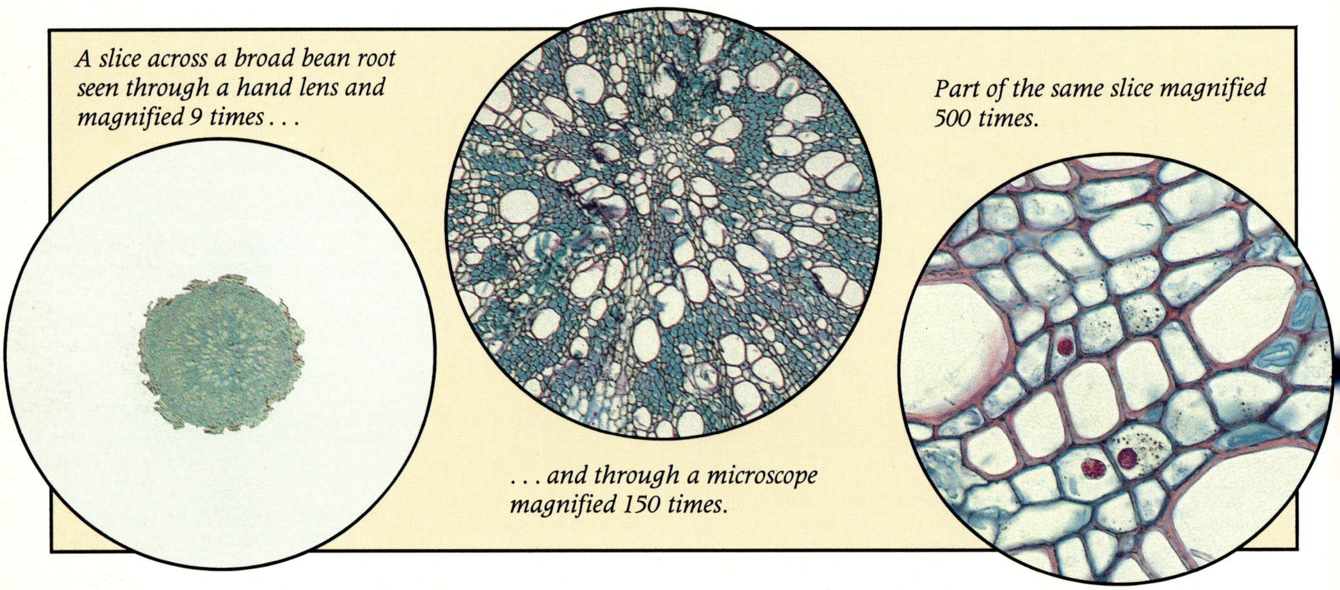

A slice across a broad bean root seen through a hand lens and magnified 9 times . . .

. . . and through a microscope magnified 150 times.

Part of the same slice magnified 500 times.

Nowadays there is an even more powerful magnifier than the kind of microscope you can use at home or school. It is called an electron microscope, and it has helped us to make a vast leap in our scientific knowledge.

The great scientific pioneers like Louis Pasteur had many scientific battles with microbes they could not see with their microscopes. Pasteur in particular developed the vital medical treatment called vaccination. To produce a vaccine a scientist must find the microbe that causes a particular disease, weaken it, and then mix it with a fluid that can be injected into a person. The weakened microbe inside the body forces the body to develop weapons, so that it is ready to defend itself against live, strong microbes of the same kind, if they ever arrive.

Pasteur's first vaccine for humans was a cure for rabies – a terrifying disease produced by a bite from a rabid animal. Victims go mad and die from suffocation or become paralysed. Pasteur was certain that a microbe caused the disease. But he could not find the microbe anywhere in a rabies victim. Three years of searching, trial and error went by. He had to guess where the microbe was lurking and make his vaccine from dried pieces of these body tissues.

When the electron microscope was developed in the 1930s (about fifty years too late for it to be any help to Pasteur), scientists realized why he never found that rabies microbe. It was too small to be seen by Pasteur's microscope. The microbe was a virus, and the electron microscope can find viruses because it shows us objects up to a million times smaller than the human eye can see.

▼ *A sewing needle threaded with cotton, seen through an ordinary optical microscope and magnified 40 times. This kind of microscope uses ordinary light.*

The power of the electron microscope has now taught scientists that viruses cause many diseases which doctors could never explain before, such as the common cold, measles, polio, influenza and smallpox. The wonderful microscope pictures you see in books, showing the intricate structure and shape of things, are taken with electron microscopes.

▲ *A similar needle threaded with a single strand of cotton seen through an electron microscope. This microscope does not use ordinary light, but instead, a stream of tiny particles called electrons.*

Planning and choosing

Microscopes can give exciting results. But a good magnifying glass may help you see more than a poor microscope. And using a microscope for some tasks can be confusing. You may see so much detail that you can't work out what you're looking at!

A magnifying glass will show you the whole object more clearly. Then you can decide what part to look at in detail. If you have a microscope, you can begin to investigate – possibly with different microscope lenses.

This is as true for studying microbes. With a hand lens you can spot the places where they grow – even the floating specks in liquid which are vast colonies of them!

First things first

Start by having a good look with a magnifying glass. It can reveal fascinating events in the world of insects and tiny animals. Or it can show you unexpected and extraordinarily beautiful details on the surface of everyday things.

Investigating woodlice

Stage 1. *Use a hand lens to locate a colony of woodlice.*

Stage 2. *Observe their natural behaviour through the hand lens.*

Stage 3. *Use the hand lens to help you find a DEAD woodlouse.*

Stage 4. *Transfer the woodlouse to a small container for carrying it in. Be careful not to damage the woodlouse.*

Stage 5. *Observe the whole woodlouse under a hand lens.*

On to the next stage

Then have a look at the same object, first whole and then in its separate parts, with whatever lenses you have. If you have a microscope, use it now. But remember, if you are looking at an insect or other small animal: FIND A DEAD ONE.

If you have several microscope lenses, always start your investigation using the lowest magnification you have; then progress to the next most powerful lens, and the next. Remember that the most powerful lens may show you wonderful detail of so tiny a part that you can't recognize it! On the other hand, beginning with low magnification will let you get the whole object under the lens and find your way around it first. (Have another look at page 8.)

So the answer to *'which is the best lens?'* is – *'it all depends'*. It depends on what you want to see. Try all the lenses, starting with the least powerful. That way you will end up with a full and endlessly fascinating picture.

Stage 6. *Place the whole woodlouse onto a slide and look at each part in turn under a microscope.*

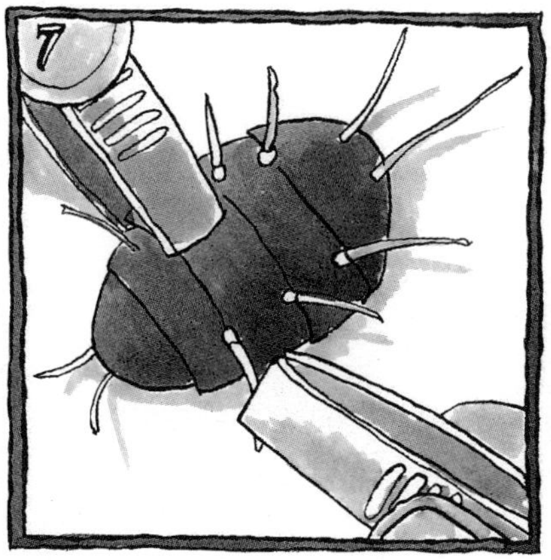

Stage 7. *Using two pairs of tweezers, remove the limbs and study them through the microscope.*

Stage 8. *Carefully cut open the body of the woodlouse. You can then study its internal structure.*

BEWARE KILLER SCIENTIST

Do not damage the environment: tread carefully, so you do not damage plants or destroy nests.

For cutting up, always use dead creatures you have found. Never kill one specially.

Never cause a live creature suffering or lasting harm. When observing one in a lens box or other small space, keep the time in confinement very short. Make sure the creature has air. Let it go as soon as possible.

First steps forward

Make a waterdrop microscope

You will need: stiff cardboard, clear sticky-tape, vaseline, water.

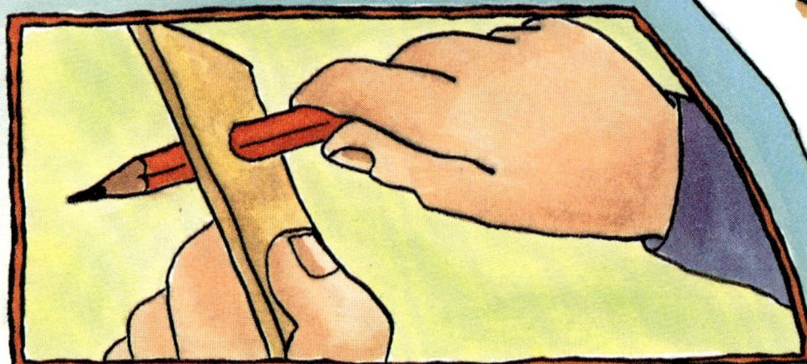

Poke a hole in the card, first with a pin, then enlarge it with a pencil. Try out different sized holes (a 4–5 mm one gives good results).

Stick clear sticky-tape over the hole. Smear a small amount of vaseline round the hole, but none over the hole itself. Put a drop of water onto the tape above the hole. This forms the lens.

Raise the lens to your eye and look down through it. Try it on something with a strong shape – like a headline in a newspaper.

Whatever kind of lens you use, the object you look at must be well lit. You must also be able to see it – not just a blurred blob. So you have to make sure that the image is clear and sharp – that it is 'in focus'.

You need to be able to look through your lens and hold that position comfortably for long enough to see what you want to. If you have to climb or lean over to reach your chosen object – make sure that you are also safe and steady.

Using a hand-held lens

Hold the lens close to the eye and move the object closer until it looks sharp and clear. If the object cannot be moved, you must move your eye and the lens closer to the object.

Lenses on stands or box lenses

Objects placed below these will usually be in focus. But if your object is very thick, you may need to raise the lens a little.

Lighting

If you can move the object, look at it in strong daylight or good lamp light. Make sure your own shadow is not falling on it. If you cannot move the object, check that the light source is not blocked. If possible, remove anything casting a shadow. Make sure you are not casting a shadow yourself. If you can move a light closer to it, do so.

Setting up your microscope

1. *Get comfortable. Put the microscope on a firm surface, (a table, bench or window-sill). You must be able to sit looking through the microscope eye-piece for some time, without strain. If you have to lean or stretch, back and neck aches will get in the way of your scientific efforts!*

2. *With most microscopes you can tilt the body tube. If you can do this with yours – tilt it to a comfortable angle for you in a sitting position.*

3. *Look through the eye-piece. Get used to using one eye without the other eye interfering. Start by covering the other eye with your hand. Later you can learn to keep both eyes open so that you can look through the eye-piece with one eye while you draw what you see on paper, using your other eye.*

Using your microscope

◇1 *Now you need something to look at! Take a slide: usually there will be some supplied with your microscope and you can buy others from a microscope supplier. Choose something you can get easily, like sugar. (You can also buy prepared slides with objects permanently fixed on them.)*

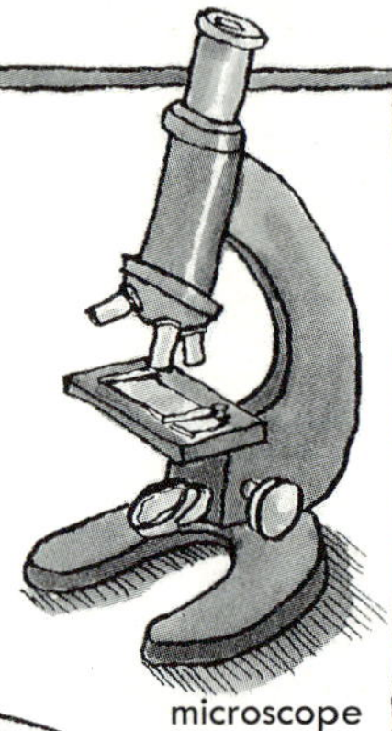

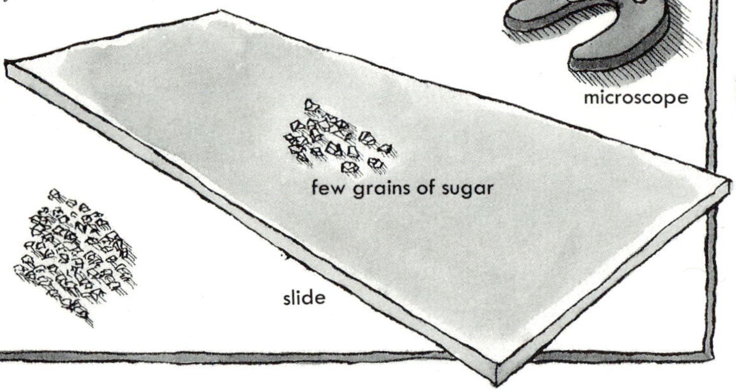

◇2 *Put the slide on the stage and fix it with the clips. The part you want to look at must be directly under the lens and over the hole, or it will not be in view when you look through the eye-piece.*

◇3 *Now light the object. There are two ways of lighting – from below or from above. It depends what you are looking at, and what you want to see on it!*

◇4 *If the object is thin enough to shine light through it, you can light it from below. Look through the eye-piece. Move the mirror to find the right angle: when you look through the eye-piece, the circle of light you see should be at its brightest, and the brightness should be even all over the circle.*

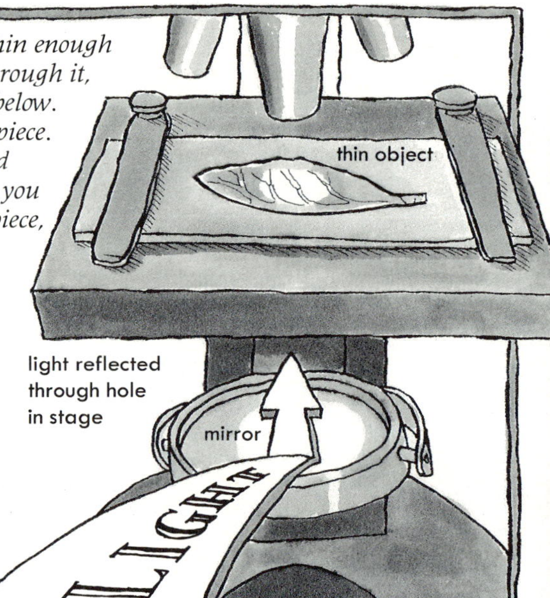

◇5 *If the object is not thin enough to shine light through, it will look like a dark shape without detail. You will need to light the object from above. Try the light in different positions and at different angles to your object. Experiment with lighting the same object first with bottom lighting, then with the top lighting until you discover which kind of objects work best with each type.*

6 Looking at the microscope from the side (not through the eye-piece), turn the turret until you have the lowest power lens in position. Make sure you feel the click that tells you it is fully in position. Still looking from the side, turn the focussing knob until the lens is as close to the slide as possible without touching it. NEVER LOWER A LENS WHILE YOU ARE LOOKING THROUGH THE EYE-PIECE. You may break the slide with the lens – and possibly the lens. You also get your lens gummed up with your samples!

7 Looking through the eye-piece, turn the focussing knob in the opposite direction until you see the image become sharp and clear.

8 Repeat steps 6 and 7 several times, until you know what the object looks like as it comes into focus. You also need to get used to raising and lowering the lens, moving slowly so you can spot the focused position for each object. Now choose and focus each of the other lenses in turn.

9 Next, get used to moving a slide to and fro to look at different parts. The image you see will move in the opposite direction from the way you move the slide. The image will also be upside down and back to front. Practise moving the slide to and fro and watching how the image moves.

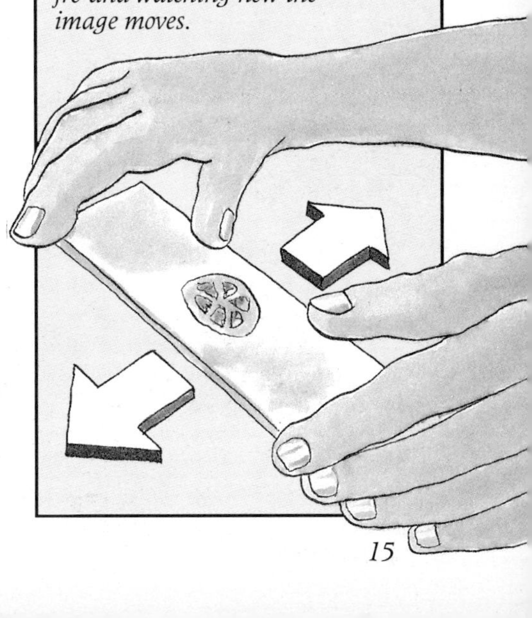

A first look

Start by looking at objects and materials you can find easily in your home. This book doesn't try to tell you what you will see. The most exciting adventure is to find out for yourself.

Practise getting things in focus. Practise getting the lighting right. Experiment: you need different kinds of light for different tasks; perhaps a combination of lights will work well. Use window light. Use lamps. Use a torch. Use them singly or together. Try them in different positions.

For example:

* *Print and photographs: compare a book with a newspaper, a magazine, printing on material.*

* *Fibres: clothes, cushions, curtains, carpets, doormat. Compare natural fibres (cotton, wool, hair), with man-made fibres (nylon, velcro, acrylic). Manufacturers' labels will tell you what things are made of.*

* *Substances and liquids: dust, salt, sugar, tea leaves, clear water, soapy water, pencil shavings, paper.*

. . . try anything you can think of . . .

Get used to using different lenses. Have another look at pages 10 and 11.

Get used to putting different things on a microscope slide. You can place some objects directly on the slide. Or you can fasten fibres with sticky tape, or trap them between two slides. Drops of water can be placed on a flat slide, but you will have to make sure the stage is not sloping or the water will run off. Or you can create a small 'swimming pool' on the slide by forming a ring with a ridge of vaseline. (You can also get special cavity or ring slides for looking at liquid.)

Are you having problems?

It is easy to become frustrated and discouraged with a microscope because you keep having problems you can't solve.

Like any tool, you must get used to a microscope. Everyone has difficulties at first. Learn to recognize these common problems and how to correct them.

When you look through the eyepiece with the mirror reflecting light up through the stage, you cannot see any circle of light.

Your lens and the body tube are probably not in line with each other. Turn the turret until you hear it click properly into place.

You can't get a bright image at all. ▼

You may be using lighting from below for something that is too thick. Try lighting it from above.

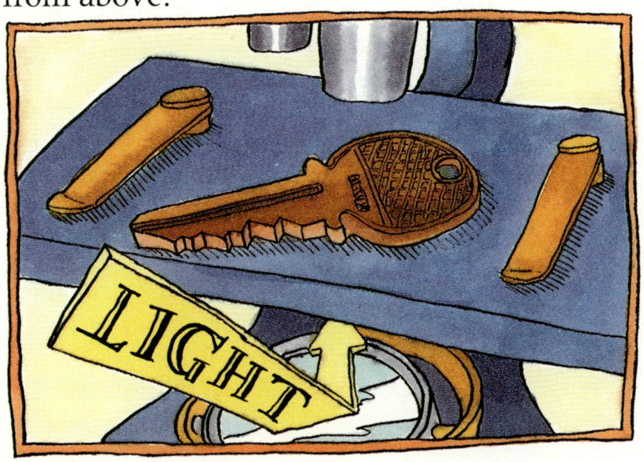

There are tree trunks and large round balloons in view. ▶

You're probably looking at dust or air bubbles or water droplets. If there are too many, start again with a clean slide and a new piece of the object.
(To check what dust and air bubbles look like, put some on an empty slide: trap air bubbles in water between two slides.)

Your image goes dim. ▼

Your reflector mirror or light source may have been knocked out of position. Your light source may be blocked. Check and adjust both and try again.

You can't find the image. Or you lose it, and can't find it a second time.

You may have moved the slide: the tiniest movements can take an image right out of view. Move the slide tiny amounts to and fro until you find the image again. Or you may be moving too fast through the focussing range. Repeat the process of focussing, turning the knob very slowly. If your object is thick, different parts will be in focus at different times as you turn the knob. Focus slowly to detect the parts as they move in and out of focus. Select the one you want, and focus on it again.

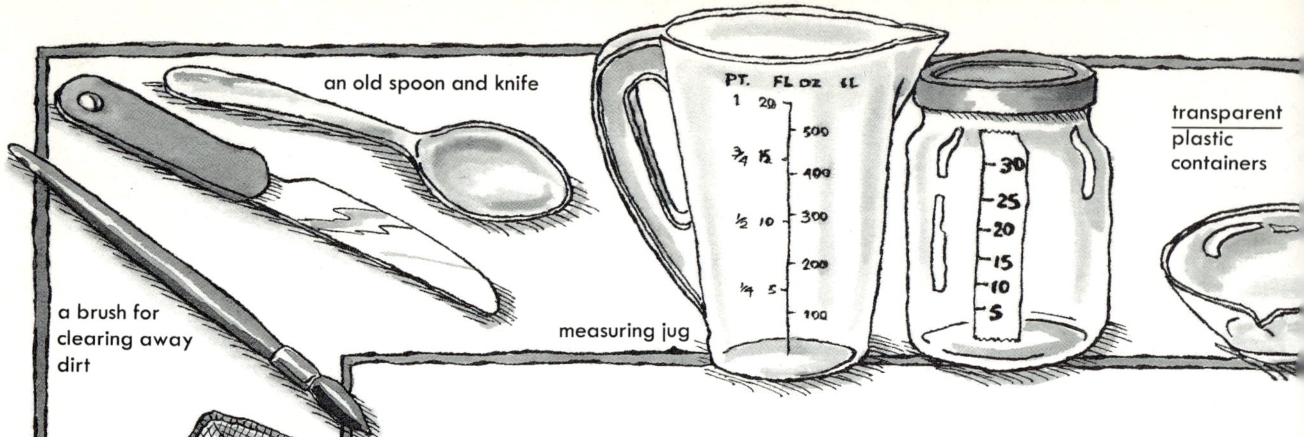

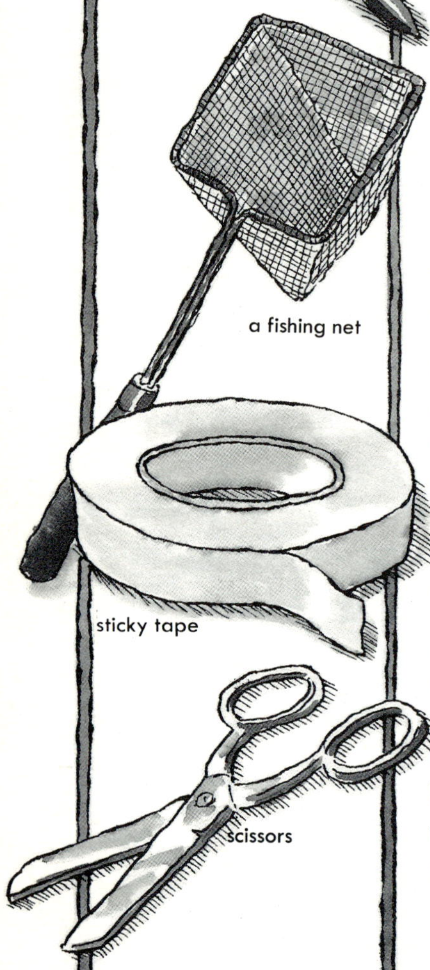

Getting organized

There is nothing more frustrating than seeing something interesting, searching desperately for equipment you can't find, and discovering that the fascinating object has disappeared by the time you return!

So get your equipment organized from the beginning. All the items pictured here will be useful at some stage in your explorations. Most of it can be found at home or bought in ordinary shops. Many microscope kits have useful items as well as a microscope, or you can obtain them from specialist microscope suppliers. (For more information see pages 46 to 48.)

It can be very useful to have the kind of specialist equipment used in laboratories. But it is not at all necessary. The pioneers did not have ready-made equipment, specially designed for their purposes. They had to invent their tools, using whatever bits and pieces they had. Remember that it was with these that they made some of the discoveries that changed the course of science.

Arranging your work-space

You need a clear surface to work on. And you need enough space around your lens to lay out the objects you want to investigate, the equipment for handling them, and a notepad and pencil. You also want to be able to reach the rest of your stored equipment easily.

Looking after and storing equipment

You also need dry, clean space to store everything. This could be drawers and cupboards, or just labelled shoeboxes with lids. But remember:

* Keep your equipment together: you want to find it easily when you need it – not three days later!

* Keep it free from dust, grease and dirt: dust and grease will prevent you seeing through the lenses and grit will scratch them.

* Prevent it from being damaged: this includes keeping it dust- and moisture-free.

* Have space for notebooks, drawing, photos, any other records you want to keep, as well as reference books.

* Organize equipment that stays at home – and a travelling set with things you'll need for looking or collecting away from home.

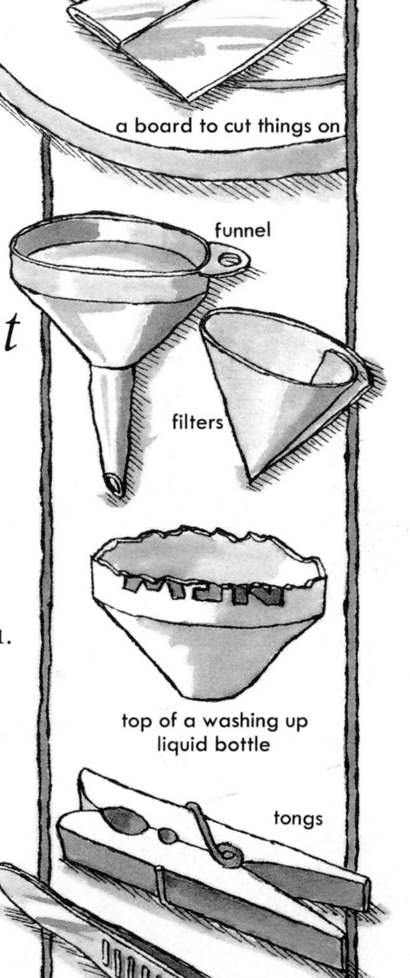

Close to home

Pick up something familiar and look at it. You don't have to go anywhere special to discover the wonder of textures and structures all around you. Look around your own home and your own body, just like Leeuwenhoek.

Collect skin flakes

Lay some clear sticky tape on a part of your skin where there are no hairs. Then peel it off. Look at the flakes with lenses and with a microscope. (Make sure you know what clear sticky tape looks like first.)

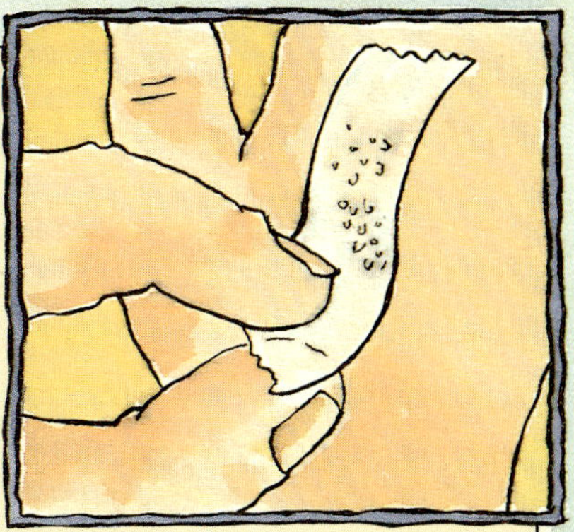

Collect fingerprints

Dust a likely surface with talcum powder. Use a soft paint brush to brush the powder gently over any prints you see, then brush away any loose powder. Put sticky tape over the print. Rub it gently but thoroughly with your fingernail or the edge of a spoon. Lift the tape gently.

Always keep alert. You never know when you might see something interesting. Leeuwenhoek made one of his most important discoveries when he stopped working to have a cup of coffee!

He had been looking at the microbes called bacteria – living in his own saliva and teeth-scrapings. His keen eyes noticed, however, that just after he had drunk his scalding coffee, the bacteria were very sluggish, or quite dead. So now he knew that heat killed them! This is the basic principle behind all cooking and many methods of preserving food.

Better safe than sorry

Microbes do very good and useful work – until they get into the wrong place. The wrong place could well be inside you or somebody else's body – through a cut, your nose, mouth or ears. All the things you handle as you look for subjects for your lenses have microbes of one sort or another on or in them. If you follow these simple rules, you can enjoy your treasure hunt for interesting subjects without making yourself or other people ill.

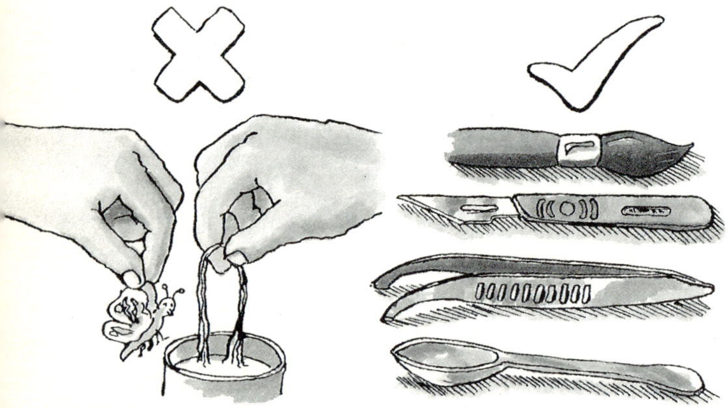

◇1 Avoid using your fingers: use tweezers, spoons or scalpels to lift objects, and prods (the end of the paintbrush or the handle of a spoon, for example) to move them gently. This will also prevent you from damaging your specimens.

◇2 Don't touch eyes, nose, mouth or ears or you may transfer an infection to them.

◇3 Keep your working area clean. Mop up any wash any spills. Wash your hands well after every session.

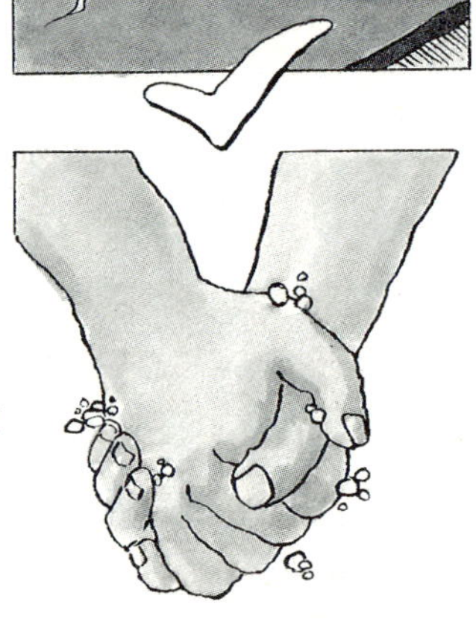

Wash them before you start as well. If you don't you may confuse your results by putting invisible substances (including microbes) from your hands onto your equipment.

◇4 Make sure you wash and rinse the tap handles so that you do not leave dirt for the next person to pick up. In laboratories the tap handles are usually levers operated by elbow, to avoid this problem.)

◇5 NEVER taste the things you are handling – even if they are foods. You may have made ordinary food dangerous by having it close to something else or keeping it in warm air too long.

◇6 Keep your equipment separate from other kitchen equipment so that no one uses a container you have used for microbes.

And remember, remember . . .

At all times, be very careful with scissors, scalpels or other blades and sharp things. Always cut away from you, and slice downwards onto a firm cutting surface. Don't wave sharp things in the air or they'll end up in someone's eye.

◇7 Never look directly at bright lights through lenses: it will hurt your eyes and may do permanent damage.

◇9 Be very careful in any experiment using heat or hot water. Never touch anything hot without using oven gloves or wooden tongs.

◇8 Don't strain your eyes! Do not stare through a lens for a long periods without moving your eyes and giving them a brief rest.

Delving deeper

It can be fascinating to watch things changing naturally over a period of time. If you watch long and carefully enough, you can work out what conditions are needed for the changes to happen. This is how science advances. People observe. Then they draw conclusions. Next they test to see if their conclusions are right – by doing experiments.

One of the most important things you can do during your experiments is to make notes of what happens, for this is how scientific knowledge grows. Scientists all over the world note down their work and circulate reports to each other: each builds on the work of another.

From interesting mould to miracle drug

It isn't so long ago that millions of children died every year and hospitals overflowed with people suffering from deadly infections by microbes. Doctors could do nothing to control them.

Yet this is a thing of the past. Why? Because now we have antibiotics. Your doctor will probably have given you antibiotics several times already, for an infection in your ear, throat or chest. Before doctors had antibiotics, you might have died on any of these occasions. Penicillin was the first antibiotic – that is, the first medicine made by using one microbe to kill another. Scientists did have ways of killing many microbes before then – but no method was safe inside the human body. All methods destroyed the tissues of the body as well.

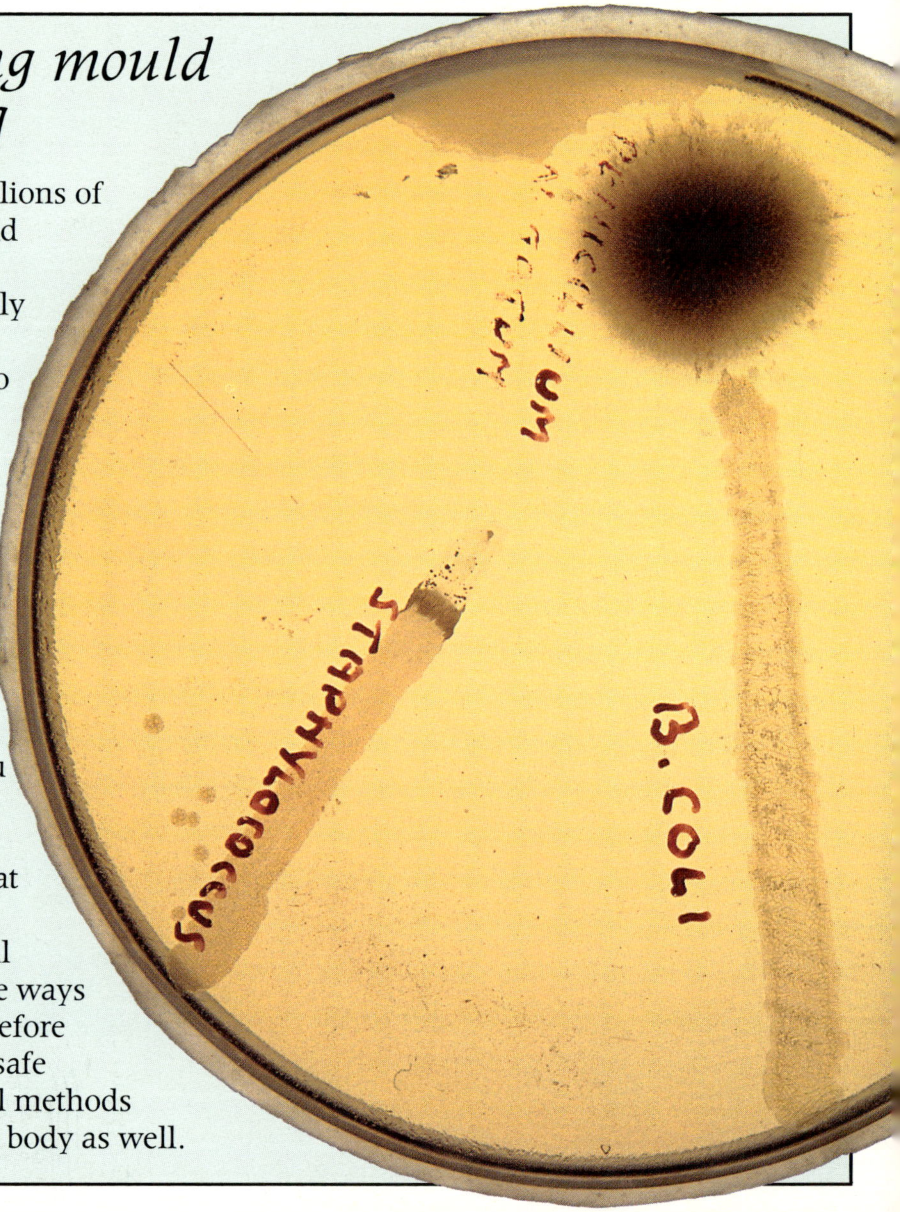

▲ *Early rewards in the battle to produce penicillin from mould juice. Florey and Chain's first batch of 'brown powder' penicillin ready to be tested on a living person.*

◀ *An early experiment by Fleming to test penicillin's microbe-killing power. He discovered that penicillin destroyed the microbes growing on the left streak but had no effect on the microbes in the right streak.*

Then a scientist named Alexander Fleming discovered a mould juice that killed microbes yet did not harm the body. He called it penicillin (because a penicillium mould produced it) and he wrote reports about it.

That might have been the end of the story – except for the way scientists record their work for others to read. Eleven years later, important advances in medicine had changed the way scientists were thinking about weapons against deadly microbes. Two men – Howard Florey and Ernst Chain – were looking for a safe microbe-killing substance to inject straight into a person's blood. The blood would carry the medicine all over the body, reaching microbes wherever they were.

They began their search for the right kind of substance, and they came across Fleming's reports about penicillin. Was this mould juice the substance they hoped for? Safe in the human body, but deadly to the microbes? They gathered a team of scientists, and began to investigate.

So one man's observation was taken up by others. And they battled, over years, in a gigantic scientific quest, and in the end they transformed Fleming's raw mould juice into the drug that changed our lives for all time.

Past, present and future

What Fleming had noticed was this: some deadly microbes had been growing healthily on a dish in his laboratory. But after a mould landed by chance on the same dish, the microbes began to dissolve. He guessed that a juice seeping from the mould was killing the microbes. He began experiments to test if he was right – and that was the simple beginning of one of the most extraordinary scientific stories. And all because Fleming never let any observation go without a closer look.

If you want to observe something over a period of time, it is vital to keep records, just as Fleming did. Otherwise you may not remember enough to know if, or how, things have changed – or your memory may be wrong! Keep your records as notes. Or make a chart. Or make an observation diary, with a note each day about what you saw.

Fleming's record-keeping was the foundation of all his discoveries. In the top half of this dish, Fleming spread penicillinase, a substance made by some bacteria to protect themselves against penicillin. The microbes grew in this area because they were protected by the penicillinase. In the bottom half of the dish where Fleming did not *spread penicillinase, the penicillin has stopped the microbes from growing.*

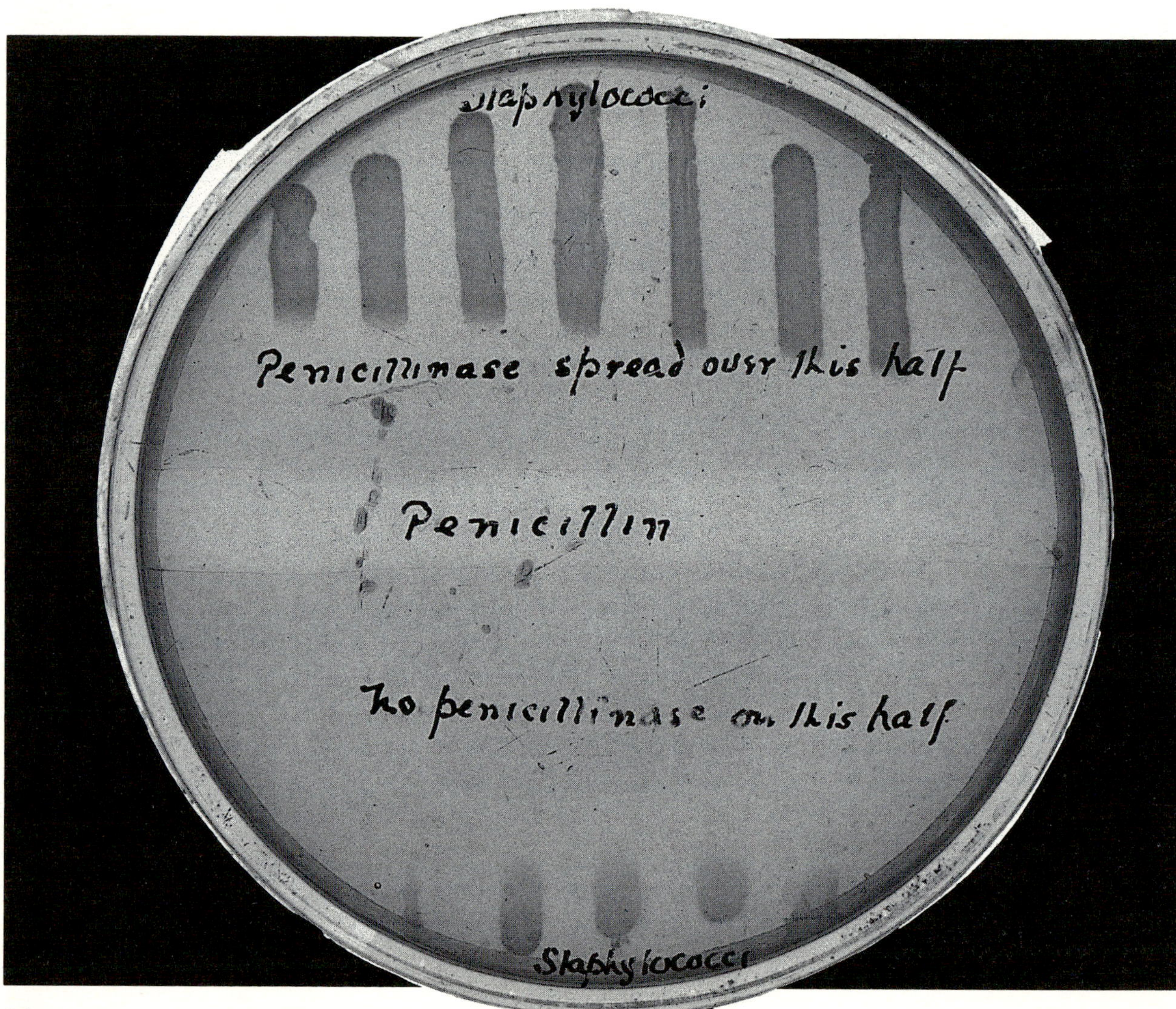

Here are some basic questions you should try to answer: choose the ones that apply to your chosen object. Add any others you can think of. Remember to keep a note of the time you looked at the object, (and the place – if your object is on the move!)

Keeping your record

Choose your questions.
Look at your object and record the answers.
Look at it after a chosen amout of time – hours, days, weeks or months later – and record answers to the same set of questions.

Comparing and contrasting

Finding the differences between things can be a fascinating line of enquiry. You've probably already started looking at different types of fibre and foodstuffs. Now do it in a more organized way.

Here are some ideas, but try anything else you can think of.

Compare animal tissue with plant tissue. Most animals and plants are made up of cells. Different parts of the animal or plant have different kinds of cells, and each cell does a special job.

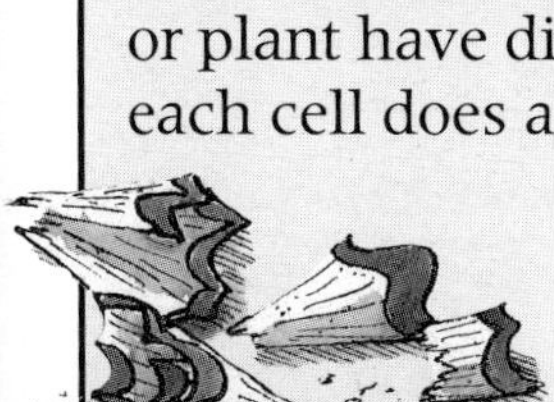

Start by looking at something where the plant cells are very clear: for example, cork and pencil shavings.

Look at scrapings from your cheek again. Under a microscope you may see the cells.

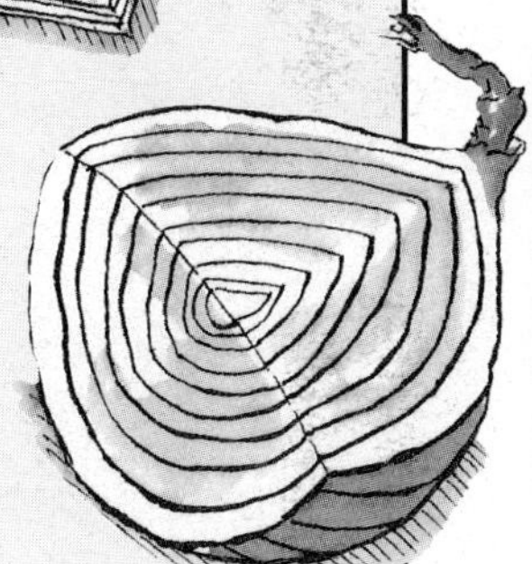

Look at other plant cells: try an onion. Look at different parts: open it and peel off the thin, soft skin inside; compare with the outer, brown dry skin.

Look at a cabbage leaf. Lay it flat, and cut a very thin slice from one side to the other. Lay the slice on its side to be viewed. This is a section.

Do the same with celery: compare the stalk with the leaf.
Compare the celery with the onion and the cabbage.

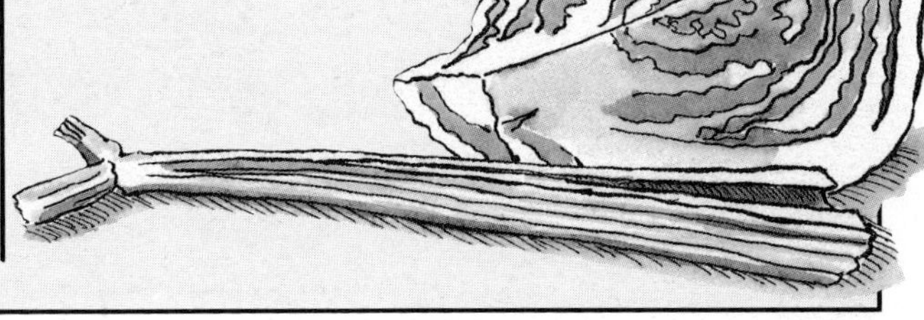

Lots of rot

Look at things whole and healthy. Compare them with things going bad such as mildewy clothing or mouldy bread.

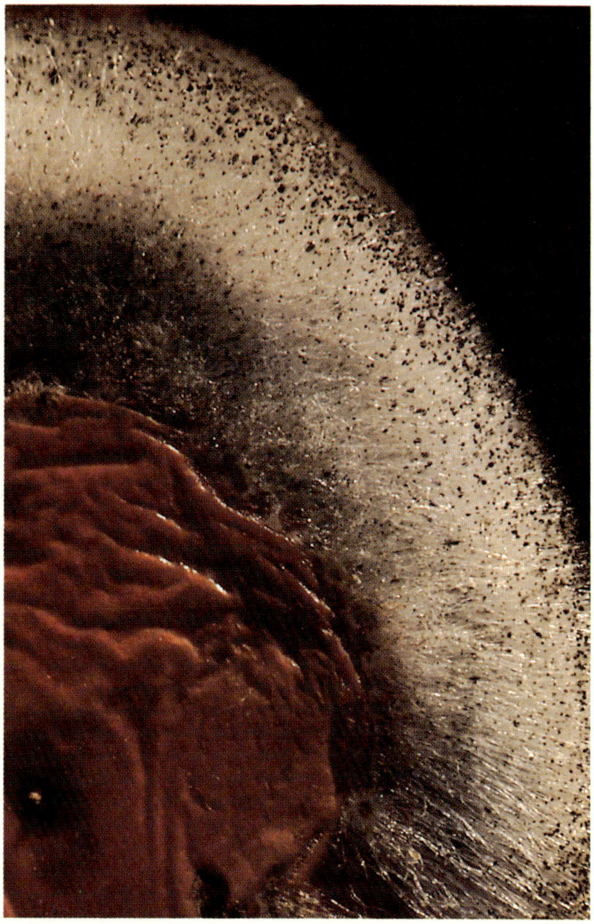

Common moulds grown on fruit which was left on a kitchen window sill (above) on an orange and (left) on a tomato.

Watch foods go rotten: an orange, apple or pear, a carrot or parsnip, old damp tea leaves. Just leave things on a saucer or in a container on the windowsill, or somewhere undisturbed. If you dampen them and then shake the moisture off, rotting will be faster. Once they begin to rot, look at the surface; slice them open and look inside. Sometimes they just go brown and soft. Sometimes a mould grows on the outside. Record the differences, outside and inside. Try all kinds of foodstuffs: you'll never know what is interesting unless you try!

Catch moulds from the air

Use raw food, such as a tomato, or cooked food, like a boiled carrot or potato; or even bread sprinkled with water. Try several kinds of food, and compare the results.

Put each piece in an open glass jar. Leave it for about an hour. Then cover them and leave them somewhere warm for a week. Start checking after several days.

Put a sample of the same thing in different places: try a window-sill, a warm dark cupboard, a cold dark cupboard, a warm, light place.

Bubble and boil

You probably think of chemistry as something that goes on only in scientific laboratories. But there is chemistry happening all the time in your home. Every time something is heated, cooled or mixed together – even when you do the washing up – a form of chemical reaction is taking place. Observe some of these with your lenses. Try looking at something very cold from the fridge – like butter. Then look at it when it is warm and melting.

Compare a cake mix with the baked cake

1. *Look at the separate ingredients – flour, sugar, salt, butter, eggs . . .*
2. *Look at each stage of the mixing. Look at the final mix.*
3. *Look inside the baked cake.*

FINDING OUT MORE...

Soon after you start using your lenses, you will want to know more about what you see.

When Leeuwenhoek started his exploring, there were no books to help him. Nowadays people have gathered a vast amount of information about the natural world. It is all there – in books and pictures – for you to look at. With their help, you can become very knowledgeable about your investigations.

Where should you start? Try visiting your local library or the school library. If you don't know what kind of book you need – ask a librarian for help.

Have a look at a general encyclopedia or the index in the library, starting with general headings.

For example, if you wanted to find out more about the activities on pages 28 and 29 you could look up these headings:

?? Animal cells, plant cells.
→ PLANTS, ANIMALS, BIOLOGY, ZOOLOGY, CELLS
?? Different microbes.
→ MICROBES, MOULDS, BACTERIA
??Chemical reactions.
→ CHEMISTRY

Experiments galore

Find out if something that happens in one set of circumstances also happens in different circumstances. Look at your records for ideas. Work out which you think are important factors in why, and how, something changes over time. Work out ways of testing this out.
For example –

* If you think water is important, try letting it go dry.
* If you think light is important, try keeping it in the dark.

But remember, if you change things to find out what happens, you must also make sure you know what happened before you changed them. This is called making a control sample: the base to compare your results against. It is no good trying to judge correctly what happens when you give a seedling no water, if you have no properly watered seedling to compare it with!

What happens to the growth of a plant from a seed if it has no light or no water? Try this experiment to help you to find out.

Grow some mildew

Try one dirty cloth and one clean cloth. Dip both in water and ring them out. Put them in separate plastic bags or any sealed plastic container. Remember to mark which is which. Check them each day and make notes. What happens if you seal a dirty dry cloth in a plastic bag?

Mouldy matters

Will mould growing on one substance grow on another? Put two different pieces of fruit, one mouldy and one healthy, close together in a transparent container and seal it. Try other foods.

Microbes galore

Leeuwenhoek managed to grow microbes in water mixed with pepper: he calculated that one drop of pepper-water held more than two million seven-hundred-thousand microbes!

Louis Pasteur had to tackle the same question – how to grow microbes in large numbers so he could see them clearly and study them easily. It all began when he was asked to help a factory that made alcohol from beet sugar. Some of the vats were going sour. When he began his investigation, Pasteur didn't have any explanation. He didn't think about microbes – because he didn't know anything at all about these microscopic creatures.

But he was inquisitive, and a very careful scientist. So he took away some liquid from a healthy vat and some of the slimy mess from a sour vat. And because he always had a long look at things with a magnifying glass and a microscope – this is what he did now. At once, with the power of the microscope, he saw the drop of liquid from the sour vat was filled with millions and millions of minute dancing rods. Yet there was not a single one in a healthy vat!

At once he was transfixed by the mystery. But he couldn't study the rods when they were muddled up with the sugar-beet pulp. Instead he decided to find something they would grow in, where he could see them clearly.

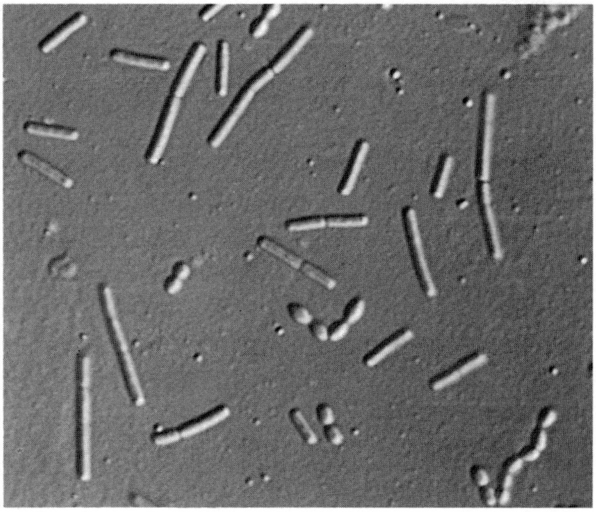

Pasteur's 'dancing rods', seen here in yoghurt.

So Pasteur became a kind of scientific cook. He tried sugar water. He tried meat soups, then vegetable soups. He tried any ingredients he could find, mixing and heating to kill any other microbes, filtering his concoction so that it would be clear enough for him to see through, and then dropping in some of his own rods . . .

Nothing seemed to work.

But one day he made a soup with yeast and sugar. He dropped a speck from a sour vat into a flask of this soup, and kept it warm. He watched anxiously for something to happen. One day stretched to two days. And then he saw little bubbles of gas rising through the soup, and specks which weren't there before. Under the microscope went a drop of the liquid. Millions of rods! From his single speck – his one colony of microbes – thousands of other colonies had grown! It was the microbes which had caused the alcohol to turn sour.

Pasteur was now on the path which led from the sour alcohol vats to the new understanding he finally gave to us – that microbes are at the root of many of the vital life and death processes on Earth.

Grow some microbes

You can grow the microbes known as bacteria on jelly. You won't be able to see a single bacterium with low magnification, but you will be able to see the colonies formed as each bacterium multiples by splitting into two. A colony shows up on the jelly as a pale blob. At higher magnifications you will see single bacteria, and you may be able to see them multiplying. They grow very rapidly, providing there is enough food and the right temperature. One can split into two as often as every 20 minutes, so that in perfect growing conditions one bacterium could multiply to more than 900 million in just ten hours!

Different types of bacteria growing in colonies on jelly.

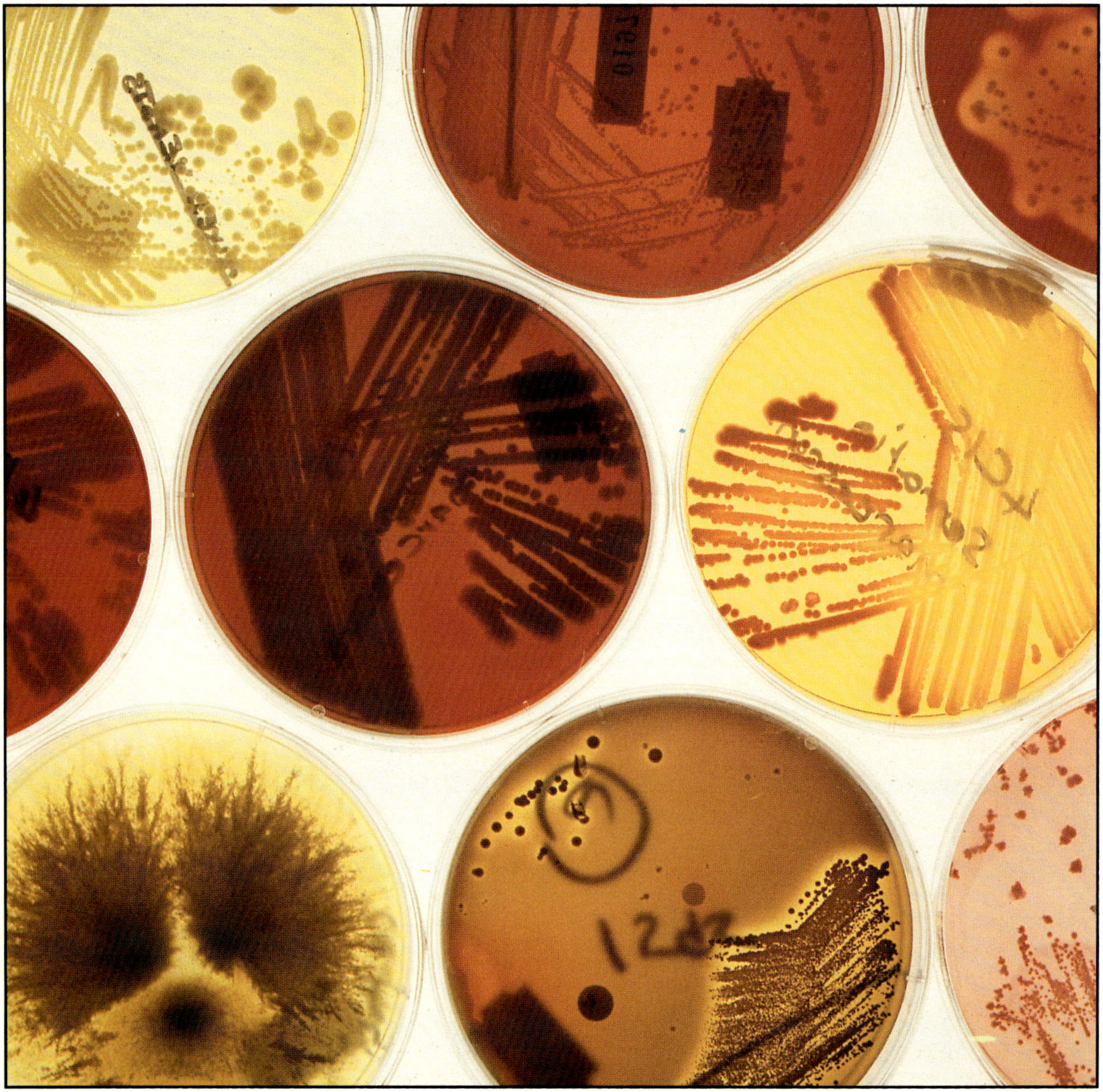

A simple meat jelly

1. You need a packet of gelatin, some left-over soup, stock or gravy or a meat stock cube mixed with boiling water to make up the quantity of liquid given in the instructions on the gelatin packet.

2. You also need shallow containers: use petri dishes or shallow lids from plastic containers (see equipment suggested on pages 18 and 19), and covers for them: other transparent containers turned upside down, or cling film.

3. Make up the jelly and pour a little into each of your dishes. Cover them immediately and leave it to set. Store them in the fridge till you need them.

Look at pages 20 and 21 for suggestions about where to find microbes. Scrape the handle of a spoon across the area and smear this lightly across the surface of the jelly. Then cover and leave in a warm place. Make sure you mark each container (write with a wax crayon on the bottom.)

Trap the microbes from the tip of your finger. Simply press your finger down gently into the jelly.

Leave a dish open and see what lands on it from the air.

You may find that you get several very different kinds of colony on one dish. Take a sample of each on the tip of a scalpel and grow them separately on other dishes. This is how scientists in laboratories isolate the particular bacteria causing a disease.

If you want to look at your growing microbes under a microscope, simply put the dish on the stage or cut a thin slice of the jelly with a colony on it, and put this on a slide.

Better safe than sorry

Remember all the safety hints given on pages 22 and 23. Read them through again.

Crystals galore

Gather some of these together and look at them: they are all crystals: sugar – (look at different kinds of sugar, including icing sugar); salt; washing soda; bath crystals.

Most natural substances that are not alive are formed from crystals. A crystal is a solid fragment always shaped in a series of regular, flat, surfaces with many sides – triangles, four-sided or five-sided faces. Different substances have different shaped crystals, and they always look delicately beautiful through a lens.

These salt crystals have been magnified 220 times and are specially lit to show up all their different sides.

Some crystals dissolve in water. But you can get the crystals back by getting rid of the water again. Heat up the substance in a saucepan. Put a drop on a saucer (or on a microscope slide.) Leave it to cool and dry. As the water evaporates, solid crystals will be left behind.

Be patient. It can be a slow process. And remember that the slower the evaporation – that is, the longer the water takes to disappear – the bigger the crystals that will form.

Fruit juices work well. Try honey. Try egg white. Try fresh milk. Try the liquid from sour milk.

The plant world

You don't have to buy seeds or gather them from the garden. Your own kitchen could be a good source of interesting things to grow and watch.

Different ways to get your plants:

▲ *Dried beans and seeds. These are all kept dry to preserve them and stop them germinating, so you must get them moist again. Soak your seeds in water overnight, so they swell up. Try germinating some in soil in yoghourt pots. If you have no soil, try with kitchen paper or damp cottonwool on a saucer.*

▲ *Seeds from fresh fruit and vegetables:*

◀ *If you have a growing plant, (like ivy), try cutting the tip of a stem with about three pairs of leaves on it. Cut just below the bulge where a pair of leaves is growing. Strip off any leaves round this bulge – and any others that will be under water. Then put it in water until the root shoots appear.*

▲ *Sprouts from root vegetables where the stems and leaves sprout out of the base. Slice off about 1 cm of the top, and put it on a saucer with a little water.*

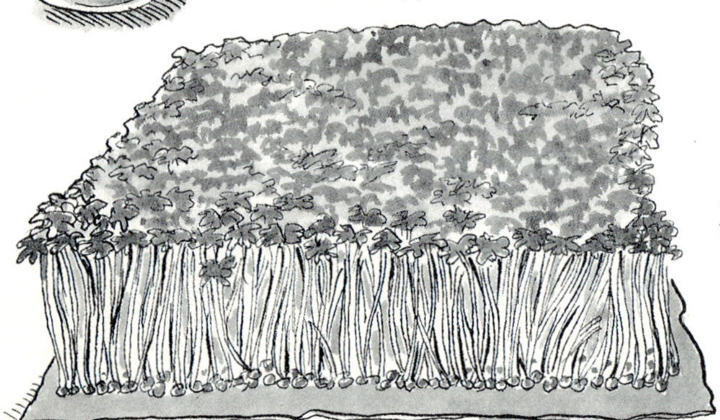

▲ *Grow cress on blotting paper.*

▶ *Put an onion, an avocado stone or a potato across the top of a jar of water, with the bottom just touching the water.*

▶ *Grow larger seeds like runner beans or peas in a jar lined with damp blotting paper or kitchen paper (or even a sponge.) Push at least three seeds between the paper and the jar.*

Watch all the changes with your lenses: see the way roots and shoots develop and leaf buds form. And remember to keep notes!

Looking inside

Leave a seed in water long enough for it to swell and split open. Compare one that has begun to put out roots and shoots with one before this has happened.

Cut up a large flower and look at the different parts.

Look inside plant stems. Celery is a good plant to see the structure – you can see the tubes that carry water easily. Put some strong coloured food dye into water and stand celery in it. Then cut it into thick slices and see how far the coloured water has travelled. What does this tell you about how stems carry water? Try the same experiment with plant roots.

Look at leafy vegetables like cabbage, lettuces, spinach.

Remember, remember...

Always have a look first with your least powerful lens. Then progress to other more powerful lenses if you have them.

Remember to get your lighting right. If you are looking at the surface structure of something you want to light the top of it. If you want to see the inner structure of it, you need to cut a section thin enough to be able to shine light through it.

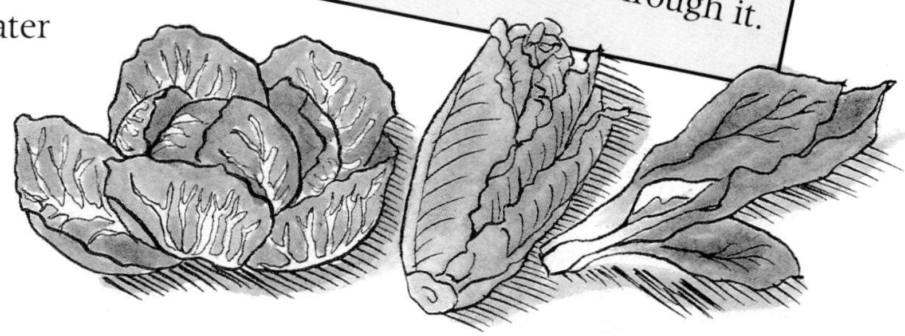

Sections and stains

Slice a thin piece with a scalpel, craft knife or razor. Try slicing several pieces, in different directions through the object. (Some things will be easier to slice neatly if you freeze them first.) Leave the sections in a dish of water until you are ready to look at them.

▼ In the laboratory scientists use stains so they can see specimens like these onion cells more clearly. Find out how you can make your own dyes on page 47.

Better safe than sorry

Never eat your experiments. You may be handling a food, but in a form which is not yet safe to eat. Some dried beans have to be boiled hard before they are safe.

FINDING OUT MORE...

?? Different parts of plants and what they do.
→ PLANTS, TREES, BOTANY (the study of plants), PLANT REPRODUCTION, GERMINATION, SEEDS, FRUITS, STEMS, ROOTS, FLOWERS, LEAVES

Into the outdoors

You may have a garden, or live near waste-ground, fields or woods, or near the seashore. Your lenses can reveal an enormous variety of plant and animal life usually hidden from view.

Have a close look at the surface of commonplace things like stones and wood. Compare healthy wood with rotten wood. Compare growing leaves with rotting leaves.

Watch insects and very small animals going about their endlessly busy lives. Remember you can also use your lenses to see evidence of footprints or droppings of larger animals. Then there is the vast variety of plants to compare – mosses, grasses, flowering plants, trees.

Here are some ideas:

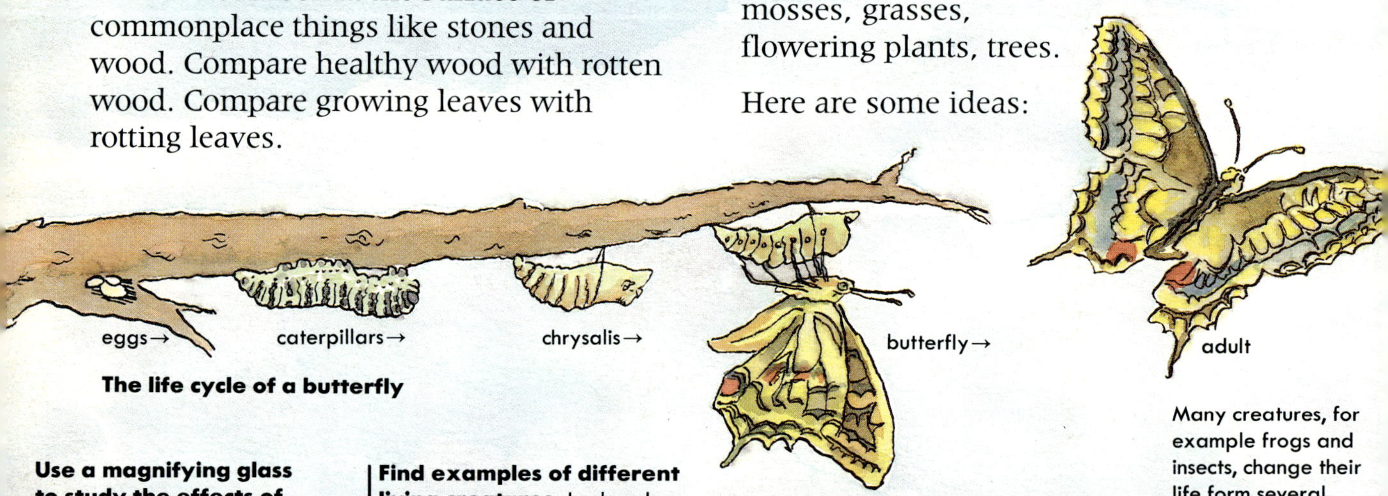

The life cycle of a butterfly

Many creatures, for example frogs and insects, change their life form several times in the course of their life-cycle. Be patient if you want to see all the stages!

Use a magnifying glass to study the effects of traffic and factory fumes.

Find examples of different living creatures. Look under leaves, beneath stones, in the gaps between bricks, in piles of rotting leaves.

Try burying things in the ground or in a flowerpot. Dig them up after a week to see if anything has happened. Bury them again. Look at them after a month. You could keep them in the ground for several months – even a year, before you dig them up! But remember to mark where you put them.

Make a home-mad pond. Put a slice of s in the bottom of a bucket. Then let rain water collect in it over a period of months.

Watch a fly's life cycle

This can take as little as 21 days. Flies usually lay eggs between June and September – so this is the time to do it. You will need: a glass jar with a lid that lets in air (a cloth held in place with a rubber band, or something with small holes in it), raw meat, sugar and food scraps. Put all the food into the open jar and leave it outside. Flies will be attracted to it. Cover it. Keep it outside – it will become smelly!

The eggs will be laid on the meat, and the larvae will eat it when they have hatched.

Remember to keep notes! In very hot weather the eggs can develop and hatch in twenty-four hours. But it can take weeks in cooler weather.

Look at growing plants and how they spread: many put out runners along the ground. What others other ways can you detect?

Find different kinds of seeds: see if you can work out out how each kind is scattered or dispersed.

The soil is full of insects and microbes – cut away a slice and look underneath. Take some to observe with a microscope.

Investigate different types of flower, leaf and stem.

All kinds of links

The relationship between living creatures and their environment is very important – it affects not only their health but often our own, too.

While you are watching things, think about how different creatures use their environment, including other living creatures. What do they need?

Here are some questions to think about:
Where does it live?
What does it eat?
How does it behave with other creatures?
Does it depend on any of them?
What would happen if any of the things it uses were taken away? But just think about this – don't do it!

The case of the sick silkworms

Louis Pasteur once had to solve a silkworm mystery. Why was a disease which was killing all the silkworms in France reappearing in a new crop of silkworms, even after every diseased egg had been carefully destroyed?

For months he and his assistants peered through their microscopes at worms, eggs, leaves, cocoons – and they were none the wiser. But they kept going, and in the end they watched long enough to solve the mystery. They learned that healthy worms were falling ill because the droppings from sick worms had fallen (from the tray stored above) onto the mulberry leaves which the healthy worms ate. The worms were infecting each other by passing on the disease-causing microbe through their food supplies – through their environment.

When Pasteur made this discovery it was a very new idea. But it is now a basic part of the way we prevent disease, for ourselves and other living creatures.

▼ *An adult silk moth lays the eggs which turn into silk worms.*

BEWARE KILLER SCIENTIST!

* **Be careful not to damage creatures.** Move gently and carefully. Remember that trapping a creature, even for a short time may cause it distress and knock it about, perhaps damaging delicate parts, like wings.

So **think carefully before you remove something from its natural place.** Only do so if you can do it without hurting the creature, and put it back again as soon as possible. A good way is to entice a creature into a jar by leaving the jar on its side outdoors among plants, filled with leaves, sticks and a few stones – and if possible, whatever it likes to eat.

* **Too much tramping also makes the soil hard and compacted.** This can prevent seedlings from growing and destroy young shoots.

* **Avoid squashing and breaking down surrounding plants**: you may be destroying nests and food supplies. You will certainly be destroying plants!

* **If you need to identify a plant, try to make a drawing,** or (only if it is a plant growing in large numbers) take a single sample of a leaf, seed or flower, or a small cutting from the tip of a side stem with a few leaves.

* **It is illegal to uproot any wild plant. You should also not pick wild plants.** Some mosses, for example, grow very slowly. You may rip up something that has taken 50 years to grow!

Zooming in and following up

Find one small area of the outdoors like a tree and the patch of ground around it and study the different parts of it in detail. Watch how it changes over time.

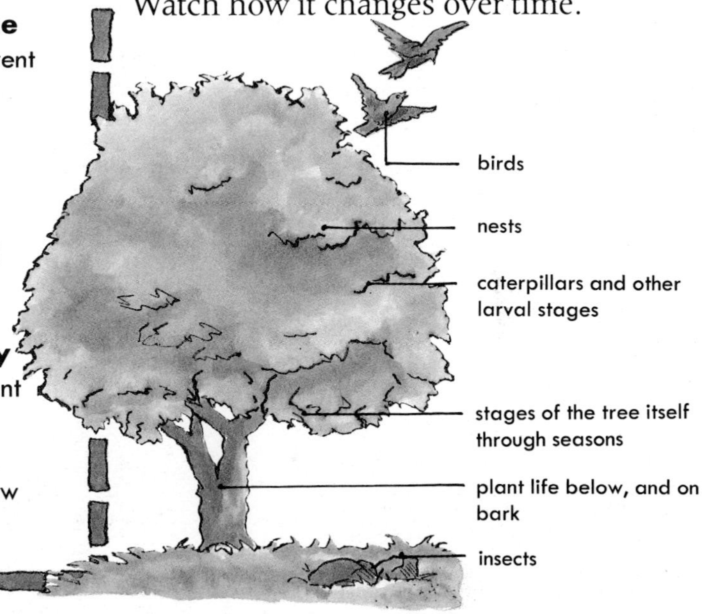

FINDING OUT MORE...

→ PLANTS, BOTANY, ANIMALS, ZOOLOGY, POND LIFE, MARINE LIFE, MICROBES, MICROORGANISMS, MICROBIOLOGY, BACTERIA, ROCKS, MINERALS, GEOLOGY, FOSSILS.
Learn to identify your finds: on pages 40 and 41 there is information about different types of animal and plant.

Further afield

The more you see in woods, fields, ponds, rivers, and seashores, the more you will want to identify your finds.

To identify a creature you need to be able to answer the kinds of questions listed below. Similar kinds of questions need to be asked about plants or trees. Prepare your own list. Remember always to keep notes, including the time and place you see something.

Here are some of the main groups of things you might see. Work out which group things fit in to. Then use your reference books to find out if you are right.

THE PLANT KINGDOM

ALGAE ▶
Very simple plants, with no stems, roots or leaves.
Examples: seaweed and pondweed.

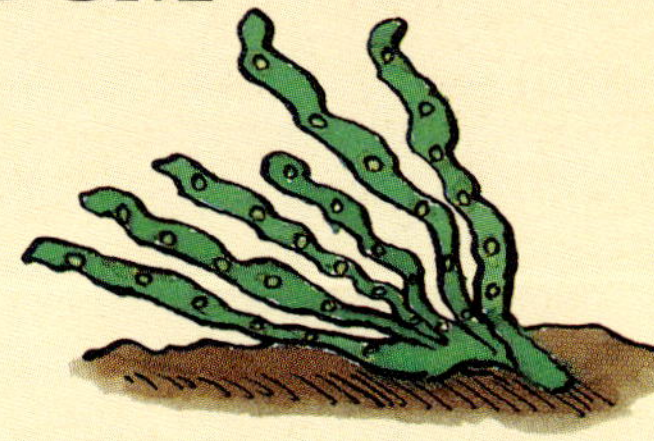

◀ **FUNGI**
A kind of plant that feeds off dead or decaying plants and animals.
Examples: mushrooms, mildews and moulds, yeasts.

MOSSES AND LIVERWORTS ▶
Very simple plants without proper roots. Grow on wet or damp ground in clusters including between paving stones and bricks.

◀ **FERNS**
Have roots, stems and leaves, but no flowers.
Grow in moist, shady places, like woods.

SEED-BEARING PLANTS ▶
Have roots, stems and leaves.
New plants develop from seeds.

◀ **CONIFERS**
Seeds produced in cones.
Needle-shaped leaves.
Examples: pine and fir trees

FLOWERING PLANTS ▶
Includes trees and flowers.
Seeds produced inside a fruit, which develops from a flower.

INVERTEBRATES

The simplest animals. The word means they have no solid internal skeleton of bones.

PROTOZOA ▲
One-celled, microscopic animals. Live in water, slime and mud.
Examples: amoeba

COELENTERATES ▲
(Pronounced 'see-lenterates'.) Soft, hollow bodies with tentacles.
Examples: jellyfish, sea anemones, corals.

ANNELIDS ▲
Soft bodies, divided into rings or segments.
Examples: earthworms, leeches.

MOLLUSCS ▲
Soft-bodied animals with shells and a single foot.
Examples: snails, slugs, mussels.

ECHINODERMS ▲
Spiny-skinned animals.
Examples: starfish, sea urchins

THE ANIMAL KINGDOM

VERTEBRATES

All animals with an internal skeleton of bones. Some are cold-blooded – which means they have a body temperature the same as the air or water around them. Others are warm-blooded, which means the body has its own definite temperature which does not vary much, no matter what the temperature outside the body.

FISH ▼
Cold-blooded.
Scales and fins.
Breathe with gills.
Live in water.

AMPHIBIANS ▲
Cold-blooded.
Soft, moist skin.
Young breathe through gills.
Adults develop lungs.
Live on both land and water.
Examples: frogs, toads and newts.

REPTILES ▶
Cold-blooded.
Dry skin, covered with overlapping scales or horny plates.
Examples: snakes, lizards, tortoises, turtles, crocodiles.

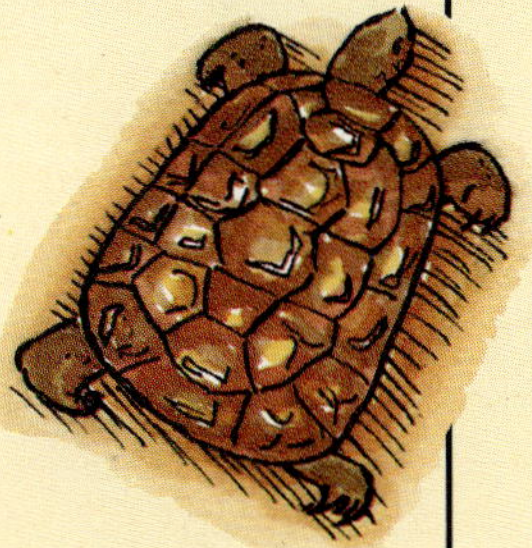

◀ BIRDS
Warm-blooded.
Feathers and wings.

MAMMALS ▶
Warm-blooded.
Skin covered with hair.
Examples: mice, rabbits, dogs, cats, horses, humans, whale.

ARTHROPODS

These have a skeleton covering the outside of the body or situated in the skin (called an exoskeleton.) They have jointed legs and antennae, or feelers. The bodies usually have three sections: head, thorax and abdomen.

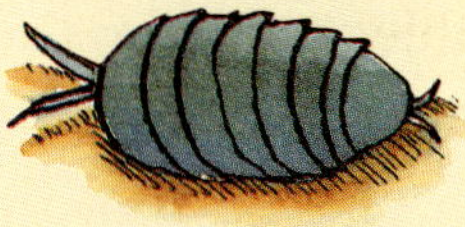

CRUSTACEANS ▲
Between 10 and 14 legs.
2 pairs of antennae.
Examples: woodlice, shellfish such as crabs and prawns, water fleas.

ARACHNIDS ▲
8 legs.
No antennae.
Examples: spiders, scorpions.

INSECTS ▲
6 legs.
2 pairs of wings.
2 antennae.
2 compound eyes.
Examples: butterflies, grasshoppers, ladybirds.

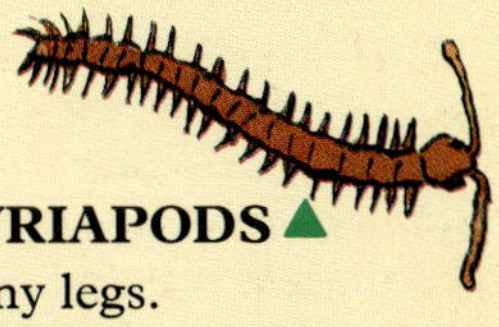

MYRIAPODS ▲
Many legs.
Examples: centipedes and millipedes.

All about lenses

Fill a glass bottle with water and stick your finger into the neck. Your finger will look bigger. Look carefully at the detail you can see when your finger in in the water, compared with when it is out.

Look at other things through the glass. They will also look bigger: try the page of a newspaper or book, or the point of a pen.

Your bottle of water is just a form of magnifying glass, like the water-drop one on page 12. It works for two reasons. The first of these is that light travels in straight lines. You can see this if you build a pin-hole viewer.

Make a pin-hole viewer

You will need:
Any cylinder or tube – a small tin can with both ends removed or some rolled card held with an elastic band and sticky tape.
Elastic bands to go round the tube, a pin, tin foil, tracing paper, black paper.

Try your pin-hole viewer first of all in a darkened room.
The image is upside down because the rays of light reflecting off the light bulb travel in straight lines in all directions from the bulb; some will pass through the pin-hole in the foil. As they pass from the top of the bulb, they pass through the pin-hole and continue in a straight line till they reach the bottom of the screen. The light reflecting from the bottom of the bulb will continue in a straight line and reach the top of the screen. So the image on the screen will show the top of the bulb at the bottom, and the bottom of the bulb at the top.

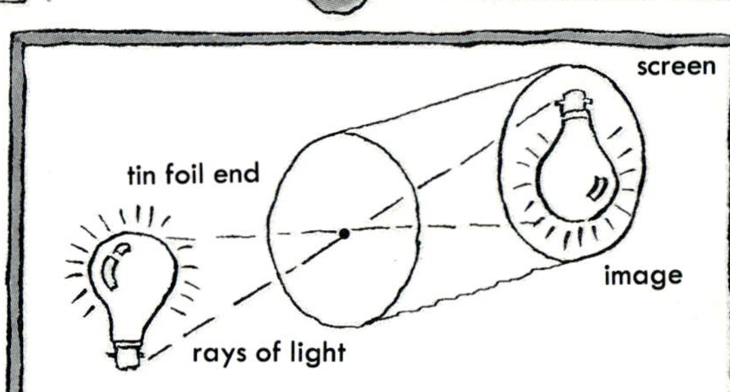

Secondly, your bottle of water works as a magnifying glass because light changes direction slightly (the ray of light bends), when it passes from air into glass or water, and bends again when it comes out, back into air.

You can see it simply if you put something straight (like a pencil or pen or a straw) into water. It appears to bend.

Try this experiment to see it happening with rays of light: you can see it best in a darkened room.

You will need a small glass container (any clear jar, bottle or bowl will do), a sheet of white paper and a piece of card.

◇1 *Fill the glass container with water mixed with a few drops of milk. Stand the container on the white paper.*

◇2 *Cut two vertical slits in the card, about 2 cms apart.*

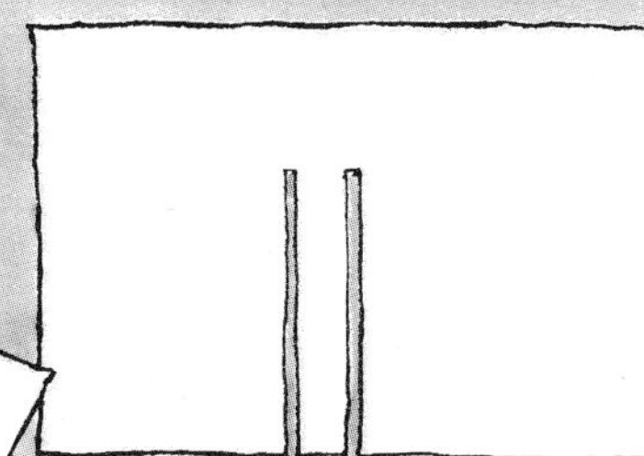

◇3 *Hold the card in front of the container and shine a light (for example a torch) through the slits towards the glass container.*

◇4 *Follow the line of the light-rays as they pass through the slits and through the water, across the white paper. What happens to the rays? What happens when they come out the other side of the water?*

Lenses

The lenses you have been using throughout this book work on the same principles. They are simply shaped glass (or shaped transparent plastic), designed to bend light rays in a particular direction and angle and give you a larger image of an object than the image your naked eye would see.

Pushing back the frontiers of knowledge

Since the days of Leeuwenhoek in the 17th century, lenses and microscopes have transformed what we know about our planet. Two hundred years later they revealed their full power as weapons for a better world in the hands of people like Louis Pasteur.

Pasteur showed us the huge part that microbes play in our lives. Some perform vital work, making waste matter decay to enrich the soil and provide food for plants. Some even take part in the way we digest food. We have harnessed others to turn raw materials into foods like bread and cheese. Pasteur also showed that other microbes cause disease when they invade humans, animals or plants.

By the beginning of this century many scientists in many countries had tracked and named most of the common bacteria. When the electron microscope was invented in the 1930s, scientists could see smaller microbes than ever before – the viruses. Beginning with Pasteur's work in the 1870s and 1880s, scientists developed vaccines against many common microbes. And then in the 1940s came penicillin, the first antibiotic. Now doctors had a powerful general weapon against bacteria in the body. To this day, new, more powerful antibiotics are being developed.

Other scientists had been using microscopes to study natural substances in the world. How are they made? How do they behave if mixed with other substances? What are their strengths and weaknesses? A whole line of knowledge opened up ways of making new and useful materials – plastics, metals, petrol, paints, glues and dyes, household cleaners, agricultural fertilizers and artificial fibres for clothing.

During the past hundred years, the microscope has developed from being a tool of observation into one of the most powerful weapons in the battle against infection and disease.

Microscopes today

In one way or another, microscopes are at the root of almost every field of science and industry. Whenever we need to understand the structure of materials, how to use, change, destroy or strengthen them, whenever we need to know the precise workings of living creatures or plants – microscopes are at the centre of the process of discovery.

Lenses are often the essential tool for preserving quality: for checking textiles, paper and printing, safety in buildings, bridges, aeroplanes and cars, rock samples in mining, preserving food, performance of household cleaning materials, electronics, waste, sewage and water treatment, the effect of farming methods on crops – in all these we use microscopes. Whenever we work on minute substances, we use lenses.

The police use lenses to study evidence: fingerprints, fibres, dirt and blood. Archaeologists use them to study the objects of the past – discovering how people lived from traces of plants and animals clinging to buried substances.

► *A scientist checks the amount of asbestos dust in a sample of polluted air. Microscopes are used today whenever scientists need to check water, soil, air and waste for microbes and harmful substances.*

New frontiers

Today's scientists are standing on the threshold of still more new avenues of discovery, particularly in medicine. With the electron microscope we gain a more and more detailed understanding of how the body repairs its tissues and fluids and defeats invading microbes. Scientists are learning to create special body substances which use these natural processes, changing or speeding them up, forcing cells to behave in a certain way. As more diseases are controlled, the frontiers of knowledge are pushed further back.

The more we learn, the more we see that a small observation in one field may have vast importance in another. Even now something noticed – perhaps in the body of a moth – may point to a new weapon against disease. After all, Alexander Fleming once spotted a microbe-killing power that changed medicine for all time – and he saw it in no more than the raw juice of a small, almost unnoticeable, patch of fluffy mould.

Some Specialist lenses

▼ **Loupe** – used for looking at film or at objects laid on lightboxes (specialist photographic shops).

▼ **Watchmaker's eyeglass** – this is gripped in the eye socket so that both hands are free for work (tool, scientific or instrument shops).

► **Stereomicroscope** – this is two microscopes – one for each eye (not just two eye-pieces as in the binocular microscope). It lets you see the object in three dimensions – that is, to see height, width and depth, because each of your eyes has a different view. It does not magnify as much as a normal microscope: the range being about × 15 to × 30.

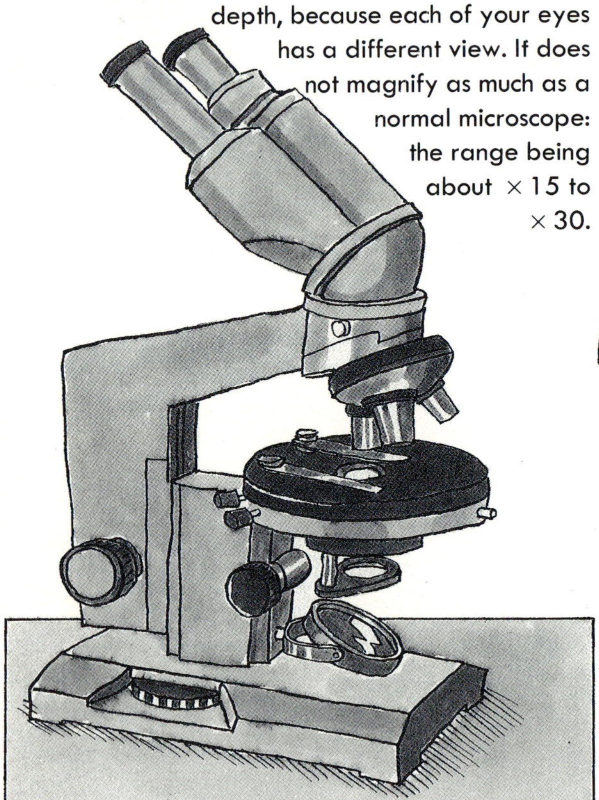

► **Linen tester or piece glass** – used for counting the threads in textile manufacture (specialist scientific or instrument shops).

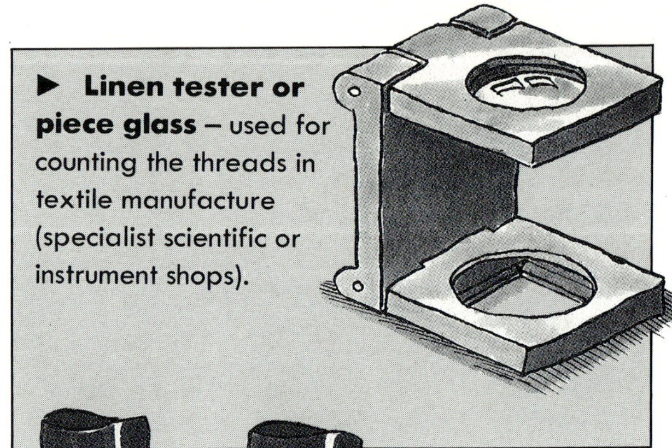

◄ **Binocular or multi-ocular microscopes** – binocular microscopes allow you to look at the object with both eyes; multi-ocular allow a number of people to look through at the same time.

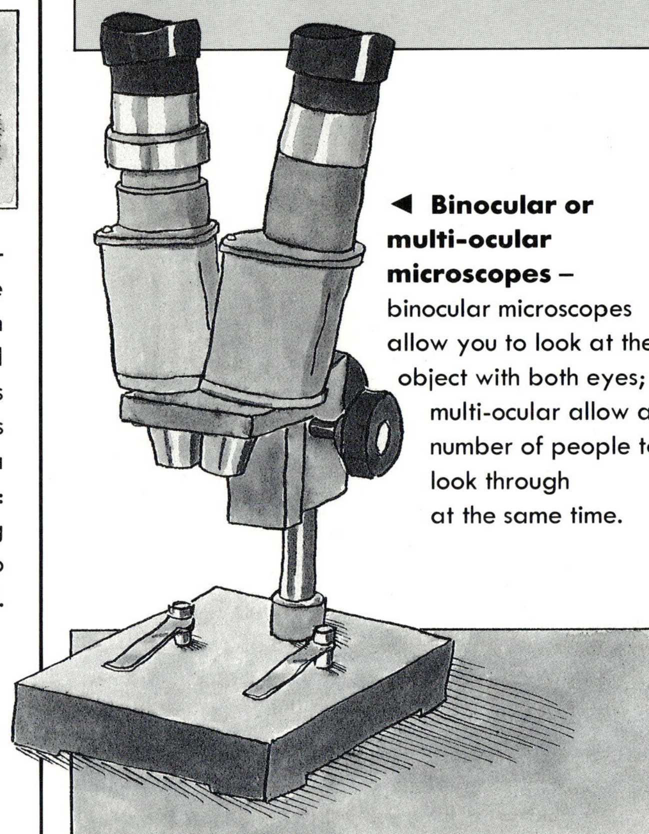

You can also fit a camera (even a video camera) to a microscope instead of an eye-piece. You can then take photographs and keep a permanent record, even of moving objects.

Some microscopes can be used as projectors. You can then project the image onto a wall – so that many people can see it at the same time – or onto a table – so that you can trace it onto paper.

Some special techniques

Stains and colour filters

Some things you might want to examine under a microscope will look nearly colourless. If you stain them, you will be able to see more detail. This is because different parts of the object take up different amounts of stain, so the shapes and structures inside the object show up clearer.

You can use food dyes. Experiment with them. Just put a small drop of food colour straight onto your specimen on the slide. Or mix up a dish of the colour (1 teaspoon of colour to a mug of water) and soak your section in it. Drain it well before putting it on the slide. Many microscope kits contain special stains; you can buy them from chemists and hardware shops too. Some common stains are:

Carmine (pink); Methylene blue (blue); Iodine (tincture of iodine) (blue or red – depending on what you stain); Acid fuchsin (reddish brown); Eosin (pink).

You can also use different coloured filters – cellophane or celluloid (bought from stationers or craft shops). Try different colours. Experiment by simply holding them above the object on the stage, below your objective lens. When you have decided which colour filter gives the clearest results, secure it in place above or below the slide. Some microscopes are fitted with filters that you can easily swing into place under the stage.

Slide preparation

There are two ways to stop a specimen drying out on a slide before you have had a chance to look at it:

Temporary mounts

Make your sample very thin (using a razor blade or scalpel). Pick it up with tweezers and put it in the middle of a clean slide. Put a drop of water on the sample and cover it with a slide cover. Blot up any excess water (with blotting or tissue paper). It is important not to trap air bubbles.

Permanent mounts

Prepare the sample as for a temporary mount, but put a drop of gum media on the sample instead of water and cover with a slid cover. Push down gently on the slide cover and leave it to dry for about a day. The slide cover will be permanently stuck in place. You can use these kinds of slides to start a slide library of your own.

SOME USEFUL ADDRESSES AND WHERE TO GET HOLD OF THINGS

You can buy lenses and microscopes at larger toy shops and toy departments; lenses and lens equipment can also be found at chemists, photographic shops, and at general tool and instrument shops.

You can also obtain catalogues and price lists direct from:

Berol Limited
Oldmedow Road
King's Lynn
Norfolk PE30 4JR
Telephone: 0553 761221

C. E. Offord (Microscopes)
Ticehurst Road
Hurst Green
Etchingham
E. Sussex TN19 7QT
Telephone: 0580 200739

Osmiroid Educational
Osmiroid International Ltd
Fareham Road
Gosport
Hampshire PO13 0AL
Telephone: 0329 232345

Science of Cambridge Limited
Croxton Park
Croxton
Cambridgeshire PE19 4SY
Telephone: 048087 452

Tasco
Sales Office
2 Tewin Court
Tewin Road
Welwyn Garden City
Herts A17 1AU
Telephone: 0707 376660

Microscope slides, chemicals, stains and information leaflets are available from:

NBS Microscopical supplies
3 Betts Avenue
Martlesham Heath
Ipswich
1PS 7HR

For a wide range ,of leaflets and posters about why we should care for wildlife and wildplaces – and how to do so, write to:

Nature Conservancy Council
Information and Library Services
Northminster House
Peterborough
PE1 1UA
Telephone: 0733 340345

Index

antibiotics 24, 44

bacteria 20,21, 32, 33, 44

cells 8, 21,27, 45
chemistry 29
colour filters 47
control sample 30
crystals 20, 33

diseases 4, 9, 24, 38, 44, 45

electron microscope 3, 8, 9, 44, 45
environment 11, 36, 37, 38, 39
equipment 18, 19, 23

field microscope 6
Fleming, Alexander 25, 26, 45
focussing 12, 13, 15, 16, 17

hand lens 6

identifying 39,40, 41

keeping records 25, 26, 27, 28, 30

Leeuwenhoek, Antony van 3, 4, 6, 21, 29, 31, 44
lenses 3, 4, 5, 8, 10, 11, 12, 13, 14, 15, 16, 18, 19, 21, 22, 23, 29, 31, 34, 36, 42, 43, 44, 45, 46, 47
life cycle 37
lighting 12, 13, 14, 16, 17, 35

materials 16, 44, 45
microbes 6, 8, 9, 10, 21, 22, 23, 24, 25, 26, 31, 32, 33, 36, 38, 44, 45
microscopes 4, 5, 6, 7, 8, 9, 10, 11, 12, 13, 14, 15, 17, 18, 19, 21, 31, 33, 36, 38, 44, 45, 46, 47
moulds 20, 25, 26, 28, 30, 45
mounts 47

Pasteur, Louis 6,8, 9, 31, 38, 44
penicillin 24, 25, 26, 44
pin-hole viewer 42
problems 17

safety 22, 23, 35
sections 27, 35
silkworms 38
slides 14, 15, 16, 17, 33, 47
stains 35, 47

vaccination 8
vaccine 8, 9, 44
virus 9, 44

waterdrop microscope 12, 42
workspace 18